Thomas Paine's
Common Sense

Bust of Thomas Paine by Sidney H. Morse. Commissioned in commemoration of the Centennial of the American Revolution, 1876. Courtesy American Philosophical Society.

A BICENTENNIAL EDITION

Thomas Paine's Common Sense:

THE CALL TO INDEPENDENCE

Edited, with an Introduction, Illustrations, and Explanatory Notes

By THOMAS WENDEL
San Jose State University

BARRON'S EDUCATIONAL SERIES, INC.
Woodbury, New York

Library of Congress Cataloging in Publication Data

Paine, Thomas, 1737–1809.
  Thomas Paine's Common sense.

  SUMMARY: Presents the text with annotations of
"the single most influential political pamphlet ever
published in America."
  1. United States—Politics and government—Rev-
olutions, 1775–1783. 2. Political science.
3. Monarchy. [1. United States—Politics and
government—Revolution, 1775–1783. 2. United States—
History—Revolution, 1775–1783—Causes] I. Wendel,
Thomas. II. Title. III. Title: Common sense.
E211.P1455 1975   973.3'11   75–28222
ISBN 0–8120–0655–0

For Charlotte

TABLE OF CONTENTS

PREFACE

IN a recent article, "Thomas Paine: a Survey of Research and Criticism Since 1945," in *The British Studies Monitor* (Winter, 1975, pp. 3–29), Professor Alfred Owen Aldridge writes, "Among major authors of English prose, Paine is one of the most neglected from the perspective of *explication de texte*. To this day there has still not been published an annotated edition of *Common Sense* identifying, for example, even such basic passages as quotations from Milton." The present edition is intended to fill that gap. Professor Aldridge should be pleased to find that the passage quoted by Paine from *Paradise Lost* is dutifully noted—book and line.

The editor confesses to finding some of Paine's allusions particularly intriguing, for example, that regarding the Terrible Privateer, Captain Death. The editor abjured the temptation of adding to footnote 35 the dizzying thought that had Pain, as he then spelled it, remained aboard that fated craft, there would have been one more apt name to add to a cast of characters worthy of the poet Spenser.

To Professor Eric Foner, who made available in typescript his superb work on Paine, go my thanks. I wish also to express my appreciation to Mrs. H. Stephans of the Library of the American Philosophical Society who devoted a good part of a day to plying me with the hundreds of items from the magnificent Gimbel collection of Paine materials now in the Society's possession.

And finally, this bicentennial year it may not be inappropriate to dedicate this edition to the memory of the most unfairly maligned father of American independence, Thomas Paine, who in the second of the *Crisis* papers, was the first person to denominate his adopted country the United States of America.

Thomas Wendel
San Jose State University
July 4, 1975

INTRODUCTION

*the end of rebellion is liberation, while the
end of revolution is the foundation of freedom*

Hannah Arendt, *On Revolution*

ON the morning of April 19, 1775, six companies of British light infantry led by Major John Pitcairn in a search for patriot military
supplies were confronted by some seventy armed
villagers on Lexington Green. Though sullenly
beginning to disperse in the face of overwhelming
odds, the minutemen, nevertheless, refused the
British order to lay down their arms. Someone
opened fire. The War of the American Revolution had begun.

The Lexington villagers who engaged the British, and the Americans that same day who fought
at Concord, were not thinking of independence
from Great Britain, much less the formation of a
new nation. Nor did the sharpshooters who turned

the British retreat from Concord into a bloody rout foresee the ultimate result of that day's epochal action. There would be nine more months of fighting before Thomas Paine published his vivid call for independence and the formation of a republic. Following six more months of debate on the issues he raised, Congress would at last declare independence and the states draw up new constitutions of government.

Few Americans, however, could conceive of such eventualities at the beginning of the war. "I never had heard in any Conversation from any Person drunk or sober," Benjamin Franklin later recalled, "the least Expression of a wish for a Separation, or Hint that such a Thing would be advantageous to America." For what, then, did the men of Lexington and Concord risk and forfeit their lives? "Liberty," would have been the reply of the militiamen. Expanding on the term, others might answer that they fought for their rights as Englishmen or, more simply, their rights as men. Still others would express their burning hatred of the arrogant military government of their colony. Lexington at last provided the opportunity tangibly to vent that hatred against the visible symbols of oppression, the redcoats.

Resentment—passionate and deep—had been building in Massachusetts and other continental colonies for many years. Though the colonies suffered deep divisions among themselves that contributed to their hesitancy to separate from the mother country, they also displayed essential similarities so that to the patriots, the cause of Massachusetts seemed the cause of America. Chief among these similarities was that each of the colonies enjoyed the privilege of a representative assembly. In all of the colonies, the assemblies had engaged in a quest for power. Just as the English House of Commons had gained a status coequal with Crown and Lords in Britain's unwritten constitution, so America's thirteen "little parliaments" demanded a similar role in relation to the colonial governors and councils.

Nine of the colonies by mid-eighteenth century were royal; that is, the Crown chose their governors in whom the royal prerogative was personified. The Crown also appointed the members of the governors' councils. These acted both as an upper house of the legislature—pale shadows of the House of Lords—and as executive councils to the governors. Proprietary families rather than the Crown appointed the governors and councils of Pennsylvania and Maryland. Rhode Island and Connecticut, under their century-old corporate charters, elected their executive officers.

From London's point of view, the governors were the essential links between Britain and her colonies. The colonial assemblies, existing only at the pleasure of the Crown, were viewed as "incorporations at a distance," empowered to make essential bylaws perhaps, but not truly legislative bodies, and certainly not parliaments in the same sense as the grand Parliament of England.

The colonies held quite a different view of the imperial constitution. Their assemblies stood guard over their rights as Englishmen; the assemblies, like Parliament, were English bulwarks against arbitrary power. They, and they alone, had the authority to grant the people's moneys for public purposes.

The clash between the imperial and colonial views of the empire had created a series of rebellions throughout the 1760's and early '70's. The Stamp Act, the Townshend duties, and the Tea Act all represented Parliament's claim of authority to tax Americans in spite of the tradition that an Englishman may be taxed only by representatives of his own choosing. During the ten years preceding Lexington and Concord, the colonists had repeatedly defied Parliament's efforts to extend its legislative authority over them.

That assumed authority, of course, extended beyond the matter of taxation. Parliament had ordered the suspension of New York's legislative assembly until that colony agreed to comply with the quartering acts. These acts, too, were deeply resented. Not only did they require the expenditure of moneys toward supplying quarters for the troops (an explicit denial of the colonial legislatures' sole competence in this area), but they also provided for a standing army in a time of peace. Here was a critical threat to liberty, a threat made manifest in the Boston Massacre of 1770. Yet "no standing armies" formed a vital part of the heritage of Englishmen everywhere in the centuries-long struggle for constitutional liberties.

The patriot response to Britain's colonial policies was loudly to proclaim their rights as Englishmen. Herein lay a rich irony; the colonials were motivated less by their feelings of differences from their English cousins, than by their feelings of "Englishness," an Anglicanization that increased in self-consciousness as their societies stabilized and matured. Why should colonial Englishmen be denied the right of legislation by representatives of their own choosing? Why should colonial Englishmen be tried in courts of admiralty (courts martial, in fact) for civil crimes such as smuggling, when Englishmen at home retained their right to trial by jury in similar cases? Why should colonial Englishmen be subjected to general search warrants—the hated writs of assistance—when Englishmen at home retained the protections of due process of law? Why should the tenure of colonial judges be at the King's pleasure, putting the court system into the hands of the executive, when English judges served during good behaviour—that is, free of the threat of executive interference? In short, the colonists did not believe that the act of emigration necessitated a curtailment of rights which they had previously enjoyed.

Those rights, nevertheless, had consistently been denied as Parliament asserted its claimed legislative supremacy over the empire. Responding to the Boston Tea Party, Parliament in early 1774, militarized the government of Massachusetts, revamped her court system, erected a naval blockade of the port of Boston, and reiterated the demand that all of the colonies provide for the regular troops. These so-called Intolerable Acts brought forth the First Continental Congress, which established a highly effective intercolonial association for an economic boycott of the mother country. The Congress, in its "Declaration and Resolves," resoundingly proclaimed that the colonists were entitled "to all the rights, liberties, and immunities of free and natural-born subjects within the realm of England." The American patriots had come to believe that over the past decade there had developed in England a concerted conspiracy against liberty, a conspiracy formulated by wicked and corrupt ministers of the Crown who, through pensions and patronage, bribed a supine Parliament to do their bidding.

It was in this heated atmosphere that General Thomas Gage, military governor of Massachusetts, ordered his troops to Lexington and Concord. On May 10, 1775, three weeks following that fateful skirmish, the Second Continental Congress began its deliberations in Philadelphia. On that same day, Ethan Allen and Benedict Arnold gained the surrender of Fort Ticonderoga, to be followed two days later by the surrender of Crown Point. By the middle of June, Congress adopted the American forces around Boston as a Continental Army and named George Washington Commander in Chief. In August, Congress ordered a protective strike at Canada. Meanwhile, three British major generals, Sir William Howe, Sir Henry Clinton, and "Gentleman Johnny" Burgoyne arrived in Boston with additional troops. The scene was set for the costly British victory at Bunker Hill, where on that bloody June 17, the English suffered over one thousand casualties, including more officers than were lost during the entire future course of the war.

As the American position around Boston strengthened, the British found themselves in an increasingly untenable position. Their supply lines harassed by American privateers, they retaliated with naval attacks along the New England coast, including the burning of Falmouth (Portland), Maine, by forces under Admiral Samuel Graves. Ringed by Washington's troops and threatened by their own heavy artillery commandeered by the patriots at Fort Ticonderoga, the British forces on March 17, 1776, finally evacuated Boston, taking some one thousand American loyalists with them to Nova Scotia. By this time, the American invasion of Canada had begun its downward turn to defeat. General Montgomery had seized Montreal in September. General Arnold subsequently laid seige to Quebec. But the weather, short enlistments, disease, the wounding of Arnold, and the death of Montgomery forced an American retreat to Fort Ticonderoga by July of the same year.

In the south, Virginia's Governor Dunmore called his colony's loyalists to the royal standard and offered freedom to all slaves who would enlist with the British forces. In December, 1775, the so-called Lord Dunmore's War ended with the governor's retreat to his warships but not before the port town of Norfolk had been razed by both British and patriot investment of the city. In North Carolina, at the bloody battle of Moore's Creek Bridge, the patriots routed a force of loyalists, thereby causing General Clinton to alter his plan of attack on that colony for an assault upon Charleston, South Carolina. A combined naval and land operation ended in complete disaster for the British during the latter part of June, 1776.

In the aftermath of Lexington, then, there raged throughout America a civil war, as British regulars and loyalist troops fought to bring the colonies back into a status of dependence upon the British Parliament. But in spite of the lengthening conflict, the Americans remained divided in their goals. Some did murmur the frightening word, "independence,"—Thomas Paine's was not the first such voice—but most yet clung to reconciliation. A rebellion for libertarian ends was one thing. But independence meant revolution in the sense of discarding the old and establishing new governments capable of sustaining human liberty.

An ideology favorable to liberty was clearly manifest as Americans had responded to Britain's successive encroachments upon colonial rights. It was an ideology that could encompass revolution, but no event, no appeal, had as yet effected that final transformation.

The King, on the other hand, had long believed independence to be America's purpose. Just as the colonists were obsessed with the idea of a corrupt ministry conspiring to devour their freedom, many Englishmen had long believed there was a similar conspiracy in America, a conspiracy for independence. Though there had been no conspiracy, it is true that as the war intensified, some Americans had come to the conclusion that it must eventuate in independence. But they had given little if any thought to what system of government would replace King, Lords, and Commons. This issue would have to be faced before they could convince others to take so revolutionary a step. Some patriots also conceived of independence as an element of strategy by which to obtain foreign aid. But strategic considerations alone could not motivate so portentous an act.

Similarities among the colonies brought them to rebel; their differences, as well as their lack of ideological commitment, militated against separation from the mother country. Some colonies, like Pennsylvania and New York, had extremely heterogeneous populations, an explosive social mix that such leaders as John Dickinson thought only the imperial connection could contain. These colonies had flourished economically within the empire. So had South Carolina. Prosperous New Yorkers, Pennsylvanians, and Carolinians might well question the wisdom of separation. Liberty and reconciliation seemed the sensible goal to many people in these and other colonies as well.

On the other hand, New England society was relatively homogeneous. Its economy, particularly that of Massachusetts, had declined in relation to the burgeoning commerce of the middle colonies. In consequence, the imperial connection seemed to have little to offer either by helping maintain social order, or in economic benefits. Massachusetts leaders such as John and Samuel Adams pushed Congress to take whatever steps that seemed necessary to maintain American liberty, steps that implied independence. But Congress moved extremely slowly. Rebellion had not yet become revolution.

Virginia's leaders, in concert with their New England colleagues, also desired that Congress assume a more radical stance. Caught in a web of indebtedness to Britain's commercial houses, the planter class as a whole, homogeneous in outlook and style, was as resentful as any in New England of Parliament's pretensions to supremacy over the colonial governments. Nor did Governor Dunmore's offer of emancipation of the slaves endear the planters to the royal authority.

Not only did attitudes toward Britain differ from colony to colony depending upon their differing societies and economic systems, but there were also severe strains between colony and colony. Virginians and Massachusetts men might work together in Congress, but the slaveholding planter had little in common with the counting-house Yankee. Could such divergent communities come together as a single nation? Boundary disputes also created intercolonial rivalries. Connecticut claimed the upper third of Pennsylvania and established settlements there. New York and New Hampshire struggled for possession of the area that would later form the new state of Vermont. Only recently had the deep-seated antagonism between Maryland and Pennsylvania been resolved with the drawing of the Mason-Dixon line.

There were those, finally, in every colony who, though they were willing to fight for liberty, were unable to countenance independence from Great Britain. The King and his ministers could be made to see the light. The demise of monarchy in America, they feared, would unravel the fragile social fabric. America's religious diversity would lead to violent sectarian strife. The mob would rise; democracy, another word for mob rule so they believed, would be the dire end result.

These were men fearful of the future, sentimentally attached to King and empire, so that they could not conceive of a final break. For all of its faults, England, with its excellent constitution, was the freest nation on earth. Besides, how could weak and divided America defeat the world's greatest military power? How could some two and a half million people, over one quarter of whom were slaves, defeat a nation nine million strong? To do so, the colonies would fall into catastrophic debt. They would become a political satellite of Catholic France, to which an independent America would be forced to turn for protection. When finally forced to make the decision for separation, some men who held sentiments such as these reluctantly agreed to independence. Many thousands of others opted to maintain their ties to England: the loyalists would suffer dearly for their continued allegiance to Great Britain.

Their position was made none the easier by the attitude of the King. As early as September, 1774, George III had come to the conclusion that "the die is now cast, the colonies must either submit or triumph. . . . Blows must decide whether they are to be subject to this country or independent. . . ." In his proclamation of August, 1775, he declared the colonies to be in open rebellion. Any Englishman convicted of extending aid to the colonials would be adjudged guilty of treason. American commerce, previously restrained by Parliament from trade with any nation but England, was completely forbidden by the Prohibitory Act of December 22, 1775. The

English navy now had full license to prey upon American ships as belonging to a foreign enemy. The small but vocal Parliamentary opposition called this action a virtual declaration of American independence. In America, John Adams, for one, agreed.

By January, 1776, after eight months of war, several congressional leaders—Benjamin Franklin, Richard Henry Lee, John Adams—had urged upon that body various suggestions tantamount to independence. These included the writing of articles of confederation and throwing open America's ports to the trade of the world. But neither Congress nor the majority of its constituents was yet ready to take the fateful step to which such measures would lead. It fell to an Englishman, Thomas Paine, to convince the Americans that reconciliation was an idle dream, and republicanism an ideal system of government.

Thomas Paine (or Pain—he added the "e" after settling in America) had arrived in Philadelphia on November 30, 1774. He carried letters of introduction from no less a personage than Benjamin Franklin, then still in England as agent for several colonial assemblies. Though Franklin's letters referred to Paine as "an ingenious worthy young man," Paine was then thirty-seven years old, years which represented a history of personal failure. Born in Thetford, England, the son of an impecunious Quaker corset maker whose trade he would enter, Paine had known little but penury and defeat. Through sacrifice, his father had seen to his early education. At age twenty-two, Tom married. The young couple lived in near poverty; Mary died within a year, apparently while giving birth to their premature child. Only three years before he left England for America, Paine entered into a second and disastrous marriage. Its failure may have contributed to Paine's desire to seek a fresh start in the New World.

The future revolutionary, meanwhile, following the example of his father-in-law, now rather inappropriately became a tax collector. The excise tax—mainly on liquor and tobacco—was hated by the people; Paine was less than rigorous in his duties and was fired for negligence. For a year he tried his hand at teaching, then was reinstated in the excise service for a period of seven years. His second dismissal ostensibly was for leave from his duties without permission. But the real reason may have had to do with his petition, *Case of the Officers of Excise*, which he addressed to Parliament. The *Case* was a reasoned plea for higher salaries for the poorly paid tax collectors; Paine had been in London away from his responsibilities while lobbying for his cause. He could not have been pleased when, at the same time Parliament denied his petition, it increased the King's budget for household expenses.

Although Paine wrote his *Case of the Officers of Excise* in suitable tones of respect for Parliament, he also expressed resentment at the wide gulf between rich and poor. Paine's England, in fact, seethed with discontent. The town of Lewes, where Paine lived for six years, was a hotbed of dissidence. And if Boston had its massacre, so too did London when in 1768, during a rally in support of the radical John Wilkes, six Englishmen had been shot down by the King's troops in the Massacre of St. George's Fields. It was in London, through his interest in science and mutuality of political views, that Paine met Franklin and his circle of friends. The cause of America, which Franklin personified, seemed similar to the struggle of the excisemen and the common people of England for social justice. Paine held the true revolutionary's belief that a change of governmental system was the proper nostrum for the ills of mankind.

Franklin's letters of recommendation opened many doors for Paine in Philadelphia, where he found a mood not unlike that prevailing in the England he knew. The imperial conflict had released the long-contained political ambitions of the rising mechanic and artisan class in the cities and towns of America. Men from backgrounds similar to that of Paine himself would lead the revolution in Pennsylvania, a revolution against England as well as an internal revolution against their unresponsive and unrepresentative legislative assembly. Their egalitarian political rhetoric coincided with Paine's political outlook. Revolutionary Philadelphia was a perfect asylum for Tom Paine, disillusioned with the repressive government of the parent country.

Within a few months after his arrival in Philadelphia, Paine had a job as editor of the new *Pennsylvania Magazine*. His article condemning slavery won him many friends who shared his passion for freedom. Paine was soon an active partisan for the patriot cause. As an English radical, he was thoroughly at home in America where the English radical tradition had taken deep root. That tradition was born in the convulsions of the English Civil War, the Commonwealth, and the Glorious Revolution, and enriched by a philosophical dialogue culminating in the writings of John Locke. The tradition was continued in the eighteenth century through the writings of such dissenters as John Trenchard, Thomas Gordon, and James Burgh. This radical Whig ideol-

ogy, harkening back to the republicanism of the
Commonwealth period, found ready acceptance in
an America that viewed its struggle against Britain as a continuation of the seventeenth-century
revolution against Stuart tyranny. The English
libertarian heritage formed a vital link between
the American patriots and the opposition at home
with whom Paine had made common cause. That
opposition to the government of George III was
of course divided in its goals. Paine represented
what we would today call its left wing. The institution of monarchy itself, Paine believed, was
the foundation of all the evils of society. Revolution, therefore, provided the only road to social
reformation.

It is not surprising, therefore, that the Englishman, Tom Paine, could publish *Common Sense*
only thirteen months after arriving in America.
He later explained that "the necessity of knowing
both countries was so material, that no person
who had reflected only on one could have sufficiently succeeded in a proposition for their political separation." The origin of the pamphlet appears to be in a suggestion by Franklin, who had
returned from England to Philadelphia in May,
1775, that Paine write a history of the Anglo-
American contest. Dr. Benjamin Rush, a Pennsylvania patriot who had befriended Paine, turned
his thoughts from history, however, to the com-

position of a work which would convince Americans of the necessity of independence. Eagerly, Paine took up the task.

The timing of Paine's pamphlet added to its effectiveness. Knowing when Parliament would meet and guessing what the King would say in his opening speech (he asked for greater force with which to defeat the American rebellion), Paine confessed that "my contrivance was to have the pamphlet come out just at the time the speech might arrive in America and so fortunate was I in this cast of policy that both of them made their appearance in this city on the same day." That day was January 10, 1776. Paine presented the first copy to Benjamin Franklin. No history this, but a scathing indictment of monarchy and "the English constitution," *Common Sense* is also a celebration of the blessings of republican government and independence.

At one brilliant stroke, Thomas Paine succeeded in putting independence into the forefront of the American debate by boldly dealing with the consequence of separation: republican government. Before *Common Sense*, patriot Americans had joined together in a rebellion for liberty. By convincing Americans to look beyond independence, Paine was instrumental in turning them toward the revolutionary goal of reconstituting

government altogether. The cause of America's
discontents, Paine argued, was not corruption
within an otherwise benign system, nor was it a
conspiracy of evil ministers. Rather, it was the
monarchical system itself that was at fault.

Paine not only composed the most telling attack upon monarchy to be published in America,
but he was also the first pamphleteer in America
to try to reach a mass audience. Political writings,
heretofore, were addressed to society's elite who,
it was believed, were uniquely capable of understanding such matters. Paine's primary audience
was not the elite, but the rising laboring and artisan class of which he himself was a representative.
Paine's genius lies in his earthy metaphors and in
the rapier thrust of his epigrammatic style, a
style that at times rises to apostrophic grandeur.
Though its introduction and four chapters are not
notable for organization or design, in its content
and as a new genre of political literature, *Common Sense* is a revolutionary work.

Paine begins with a devastating critique of the
British government:

Though we have been wise enough to shut
and lock the door against absolute monarchy,
we at the same time have been foolish enough
to put the Crown in possession of the key.

. . . The *will* of the king is as much the *law* of the land in Britain as in France, with this difference, that instead of proceeding directly from his mouth, it is handed to the people under the formidable shape of an act of parliament.

Reasoning from "a principle in nature . . . that the more simple anything is, the less liable it is to be disordered," Paine finds that the very complexity of the British constitution renders it so much more unworkable; its much admired complicated system of checks and balances is "absurd."

Having done with the British constitution, Paine next demolishes the institution of monarchy, a theme to which he returns again and again. Pages are devoted to proving that monarchy was an invention of the heathens; it is condemned by God and the Bible. Monarchy, Paine informed the overwhelmingly Protestant Americans, is "the popery of government." Nature disproves it, "otherwise she would not frequently turn it into ridicule by giving mankind an ass for a lion." As for the descent of the English Crown from William the Conquerer, "A French bastard landing with an armed banditti and establishing himself king of England against the consent of the natives is, in plain terms, a very paltry rascally original. It certainly hath no divinity in it." As for Paine, "Of more worth is one honest man to society, and in the sight of God, than all the crowned ruffians that ever lived."

Turning to America, Paine elevates her cause to "the cause of all mankind":

The sun never shined on a cause of greater worth. 'Tis not the affair of a city, a county, a province, or a kingdom; but of a continent —of at least one-eighth part of the habitable globe. 'Tis not the concern of a day, a year, or an age; posterity are virtually involved in the contest, and will be more or less affected even to the end of time by the proceedings now. Now is the seedtime of continental union, faith, and honor. . . .

The arguments for reconciliation are answered one by one. America would have "flourished" without the British connection. England afforded protection to America out of "interest, not attachment." Were America's population larger, she might be less united. America has all of the necessary natural resources to build a navy for defense; she need not fear Britain's navy, scattered as it was over the seven seas. Intercolonial boundary disputes simply prove that "nothing but continental authority can regulate continental matters." As for America's religious diversity, "It is the will of the Almighty that there should be a diversity of opinion among us. It affords a larger field for our Christian kindness." Finally, America need not fear running into debt, for, anticipating Alexander Hamilton, "a national debt is a national bond."

On the matter of the national debt, as in other respects, *Common Sense* is a marvellously prescient work. Foreshadowing the evolution of American foreign policy, Paine wrote that " 'Tis the true interest of America to steer clear of European contentions . . ." (it is noteworthy that English radicals had long believed that the King's Hanoverian connection needlessly dragged England into continental broils). He suggests a "Continental Conference" to frame a constitution for the republic—a forecast of the Constitutional Convention of 1787—and the sending overseas of a "manifesto . . . , setting forth the miseries we have endured. . . ."—a before-the-fact description of the Declaration of Independence. Indeed, America could not hope for foreign aid without first separating from Britain. Neither France nor Spain will send assistance "if we intend to use it to repair the breach." Paine also put into classic form the popular notion of the mission of America:

O ye that love mankind; Ye that dare oppose not only the tyranny but the tyrant, stand forth! Every spot of the old world is overrun with oppression. Freedom hath been hunted round the globe. Asia and Africa have long expelled her. Europe regards her like a stranger, and England hath given her warning to depart. O receive the fugitive, and prepare in time an asylum for mankind.

In such passionate utterances as these, logic gives way to emotion. Common sense dictates independence; so does sentiment: "The blood of the slain, the weeping voice of nature cries, 'TIS TIME TO PART." "As well can the lover forgive the ravisher of his mistress, as the continent forgive the murders of Britain."

Paine magnificently put the case for independence; he also expressed something of the burning anger and indignation felt by the poor and dispossessed working people of England whose cause he viewed as one with America's. Imbued with a kind of exquisite rage against the system, Paine brought Americans to similarly intense feelings, feelings which had heretofore lain dormant. His bold attack against the King may have also released subliminal resentments of the "sons of liberty" against the "father of his people"; the ritualistic destruction of the statues of the King following July 4 is a fulfillment of Paine's literary destruction of "the hardened, sullen-tempered Pharoh of England." "But where, say some, is the king of America? I'll tell you, friend, he reigns above, and doth not make havoc of mankind like the Royal Brute of Britain."

Of equal importance with Paine's stunning attack upon kingship is his insistence that republicanism is the only system of government capable of preserving liberty. Paine urged upon his adopted countrymen state constitutions similar to that of Pennsylvania with its unicameral legislature and weak executive. Paine believed that in republican government property should be given no special privilege in the apportionment of the legislature. Some men would disagree with Paine's brand of democratic republicanism, but in turning the debate to the nature of the new governments to be established, *Common Sense* cleared away a major obstacle to independence.

Common Sense, wrote one contemporary, "passed through the continent like an electric spark." In three months' time, the work attained a circulation of over 120,000 copies, comparable to a sale of ten million today. It has been called the single most influential political pamphlet ever published in America. Franklin wrote of the pamphlet's "prodigious effects." "A few more such flaming arguments, as were exhibited at Falmouth and Norfolk," wrote Washington, "added to the sound doctrine and unanswerable reasoning contained in the pamphlet *Common Sense,* will not leave numbers at a loss to decide upon the propriety of a separation." In a similar fiery metaphor, Edmund Randolph wrote that "this pamphlet put the torch to combustibles."

John Adams applauded Paine's "nervous and manly style," and his independence doctrine. "People," he wrote, "speak of it with rapturous praise." But Adams detested Paine's surfeit of democracy. Where are checks and balances, where are protections for property in Paine's wild-eyed scheme? Adams entered the debate that Paine had invited with *Thoughts on Government,* which posited a more elitist republicanism than that envisioned by Paine. Adams was not alone in criticizing the democratic dogma of *Common Sense.* But Paine had clearly succeeded in forcing others to accept independence by looking beyond it.

Common Sense went through an incredible twenty-five editions; the many replies to it only served to heighten its visibility. The contemporary historian, David Ramsey, observed that:

> *Common Sense* produced surprising effects. Many thousands were convinced, and were led to approve and long for a separation from the Mother Country. Though that measure,

a few months before, was not only foreign
from their wishes, but the object of their abhorrence, the current suddenly became so
strong in its favor, that it bore down all opposition.

By May, several state and county conventions sent
instructions to Congress for independence. Hesi-
tant or backward colonial governments such as
that of Pennsylvania had been superseded by
new revolutionary governments. On June 7, Virginia's Richard Henry Lee in Congress offered
his resolution for independence, and although
some members of Congress held back, on July 2
the momentous decision was made. On the 4th,
Congress approved Jefferson's great Declaration.

Common Sense was by no means Paine's only
contribution to his adopted country. Under the
pseudonym, "The Forrester," he replied to the
Tory William Smith's "Cato" letters which
strongly defended the idea of Anglo-American
reconciliation. Warning against "Cato's" efforts to
divide the colonies, Paine insisted "that the great
business of the day is continental." And "the Forrester" found yet another term with which to
revile George III—"sceptered savage." Far more
important, he authored the *Crisis Papers*, thirteen
in all, the first one beginning with the memorable
lines, "These are the times that try men's souls.

The summer soldier and the sunshine patriot will, in this crisis, shrink from the service of his country; but he that stands it *now*, deserves the love and thanks of man and woman." The *Crisis Papers*' widespread distribution upheld morale during some of the most difficult years of the war.

Paine further served the American cause during the war and Confederation years. For almost two years, he was Secretary to Congress' Committee for Foreign Affairs. With John Laurens, he made a successful trip to France to obtain further aid for the American war. He himself gave a generous part of his meager earnings in America to the relief of Washington's army. Consistent with the doctrine of *Common Sense*, Paine's view was continental; he vociferously supported the Bank of North America (precursor to Hamilton's Bank of the United States), urged Virginia to cede her vast western lands to the Confederation, and attempted to sway recalcitrant Rhode Island to support measures designed to strengthen the union.

Politics, however, did not monopolize Paine's time, much of which he devoted to science and invention. His was, in Franklin's term, "an Age of Experiments," and he shared with such Americans as Franklin and Jefferson and their English and European counterparts a passion for the discovery of natural laws, laws which these men were convinced could be applied to the benefit of mankind. Interested like Franklin in the principles of convection, Paine attempted to create a smokeless candle, having a second bore parallel to that for the wick. He also worked on a new type of crane, a wheel with a concentric rim, and a device for using gunpowder to power a motor.

His most important contribution, however, was his design for a cast iron single-arch bridge of enormous span whose arch segments were uniquely structured on the pattern of a spider's web. Prefabricated (another innovation) in thirteen sections—representing the thirteen states—Paine designed his bridge specifically for the American environment where river ice damaged the conventional pier-supported structures. Paine's conception typically represented the pragmatic application of theory. As a "child of Common Sense,"—his term—the bridge would create physically the more perfect union for which his great pamphlet argued.

The Pennsylvania Assembly, though interested in Paine's thirteen-foot bridge model—he hoped first to span the Schuylkill River at Philadelphia —could not come up with the great sum of money demanded by so grandiose a project. At Franklin's suggestion, therefore, Paine in 1787 carried his ponderous model across the Atlantic to France, where he hoped his "pontifical works," as he referred to his bridge, would receive the applause there given his political works.

For the next few years, Paine fruitlessly dragged his iron bridge model back and forth across the channel, seeking backing in both England and France, where he did win the endorsement of the prestigious Academy of Sciences. Though Paine ultimately failed in his struggle for financial support, others copied his design; a Paine-like bridge was built over the Wear River near Sunderland, England, and through its example, Paine exercised important influence in future bridge construction. His bridge "became the prototype," it has been said, "of the modern steel arch."

Though Paine may have hoped to create a transportation revolution with his bridge, he arrived in France on the eve of a political revolution which would turn his—and the world's—attention once more to the dethronement of kings and the establishment of liberty. When his friend Edmund Burke published his conservative manifesto, *Reflections on the French Revolution*, Paine replied with his *Rights of Man*, a work with which he emerged as the foremost revolutionary propagandist in the English language.

Bridge over the River Wear, completed 1796 utilizing the design and materials of Paine's model. A principal decorative figure of Sunderland pottery, the bridge had a span of 236 and a height of 100 feet. Paine never received compensation which he demanded for the use of his invention. Courtesy of the Gimbel Collection, American Philosophical Society.

Engraving by I. Cruikshank. Published; London, 1792. Like "A Sure Cure for all Paines," opposite, this is one of many anti-Paine caricatures published in England following Paine's trial and proscription in his native country and the fugitive's active role in and support of the French Revolution. In his right hand, Paine upholds the *Rights of Man*, *Common Nonsense*, and "equality of property." He radiates rebellion, treason, perjury, atheism, and other un-English qualities, while on his back he carried "Levelling Instruments." In his left hand is a dagger. He trods upon morality, obedience to the laws, and Magna Carta among other English virtues. Courtesy of the Gimbel Collection, American Philosophical Society.

A Sure Cure for all Paines or
The Rights of Man has got his Rights

Courtesy of the Gimbel Collection, American Philosophical Society.

Paine hoped that the *Rights of Man* would do for England what *Common Sense* had accomplished for America: the overthrow of the monarchy and the establishment of republican government. Suppressed by the authorities, the *Rights of Man* nevertheless enjoyed a tremendous surreptitious circulation. Indicted for seditious libel, Paine would have stood trial, but receiving the news that he had been elected to the French National Convention, he embarked for France. There, an honored "citizen of the world," in his native country he was convicted in absentia, proscribed, and his works outlawed.

In the Convention, Paine allied himself with the moderate party, the Gironde, and when he cast his vote to spare the life of the King, he incurred the wrath of Marat and the Jacobins. These men, upon taking power under the leadership of Robespierre, loosed a reign of terror against their opponents. Many of Paine's Girondist friends were sent to the guillotine; Paine himself, under a statute proscribing persons of English birth, was imprisoned for one year. While in prison, from which daily he feared he would be carted off to the "national razor," Paine began work on his great book, *The Age of Reason*, an eloquent expression of the deist faith, and an excoriation of Christian fundamentalism.

Paine's attack upon Christianity helped destroy his reputation in America. Though *The Age of Reason* begins, "I believe in one God, and no more; and I hope for happiness beyond this life," Paine's alleged irreligion became notorious—even one hundred years later, Theodore Roosevelt could refer to Paine as "that filthy little atheist." It was bad enough for Paine seemingly to attack the Heavenly Father, but Paine also chose to denounce the Father of his Country.

George Washington, Paine believed, lifted not so much as a presidential finger to free him from a French prison. Nor did Paine approve of the President's domestic or foreign policies, breeding monopolies at home, and perfidy abroad. Jay's Treaty, "a barefaced treachery," particularly galled Paine as "a countertreaty" to America's preexisting treaty with France. His published *Letter to George Washington* concludes,

And as to you, Sir, treacherous in private friendship (for so you have been to me, and that in the day of danger) and a hypocrite in public life, the world will be puzzled to decide whether you are an apostate or an impostor; whether you have abandoned good principles, or whether you ever had any.

MAD TOM in A RAGE

A Federalist caricature of Paine following his return to America, where, in manuscripts such as he carries in his pockets, he excoriated the Federalist Party and loudly supported the Jeffersonians. Here, with the Devil's help and the American eagle's objections, Paine undertakes the toppling of the federal government. Courtesy of the Gimbel Collection, American Philosophical Society.

This intemperate blast completed the destruction of Paine's reputation in the United States.

Paine briefly returned to his restored seat in the National Convention following his release from prison. In the winter of 1795–96, he penned his last great pamphlet, *Agrarian Justice*. His experiences in the French Revolution may have forced him to question whether political reform alone is adequate to the amelioration of mankind's social problems. "The contrast of affluence and wretchedness continually meeting and offending the eye," Paine wrote, "is like dead and living bodies chained together." Paine anticipated *Progress and Poverty* of Henry George not only in his description of society, but also in his solution for society's ills. *Agrarian Justice* suggests a single land tax, the proceeds for which would support a kind of social security system.

Paine finally returned to America in 1802—he had been out of that country for fifteen years—when the short-lived Anglo-French Treaty of Amiens made it safe for the English fugitive to cross the Atlantic. He was then sixty-five years old. Jefferson, now President, to his credit showed Paine respect and courtesy, despite the embarrassment his friendship could cause the Jeffersonian-Republican Party.

Never able long to retire from the field of battle, Paine excoriated the Federalists in his *Letters to the Citizens of the United States*. John Adams, for example, became a victim of Paineite invective. "Some people," wrote Paine, "talk of impeaching" the ex-president. "I would keep him to make fun of," Paine continues. "He will then answer one of the ends for which he was born. . . ." Paine's virulent political tracts and his alleged atheism caused respectable society to shun the old revolutionary. He ended his years fruitlessly petitioning Congress for money and increasingly drowning his loneliness in alcohol.

Paine died in poverty on June 8, 1809. He was buried in a corner of his farm in New Rochelle, a farm granted him years before by the New York legislature for his wartime services. Ten years later, Paine's bones were dug up and carried to England by his one-time critic, now repentant admirer, William Cobbett. Cobbett hoped to provide a fitting memorial to the great revolutionary; instead, upon Cobbett's death, Paine's coffin containing his remains passed in 1844 to a furniture dealer. There, the trail ends.

In his will, Thomas Paine identified himself first and foremost as, author of the work entitled 'Common Sense,' written in Philadelphia, in 1775, and published in that city the beginning of January, 1776, which awakened America to a declaration of independence on the fourth of July following, which was as fast as the work could spread through such an extensive country.

If there is exaggeration here, the old man might well be pardoned for it. *Common Sense* channeled the great debate inevitably toward the independence his republican prescription demanded.

John Adams, though originally admiring the spirit of *Common Sense*, said then that he believed that Paine was better at pulling down than building up. He disliked Paine's excess of democracy; not long after Paine had publicly reviled him, the cantankerous New Englander looked back upon the career of "that disastrous meteor" and upon the age to which Paine had given the name, Reason. To a correspondent, Adams wrote in 1805,

I am willing you should call this the Age of Frivolity, as you do: and would not object if you had named it the Age of Folly, Vice, Frenzy, Fury, Brutality, Demons, Bonaparte, Tom Paine, or the Age of the burning Brand from the bottomless Pit: or anything but the Age of Reason. I know not whether any man in the world has had more influence on its inhabitants or affairs for the last thirty years than Tom Paine. There can be no severer satire on the age. For such a mongrel between pigs and puppy, begotten by a wild boar on a bitch wolf, never before in any age of the world was suffered by the poltroonery of mankind to run through such a career of mischief. Call it then the Age of Paine. He deserves it much more than the courtesan who was consecrated to represent the goddess in the temple at Paris, and whose name Tom has given to the Age. The real intellectual faculty has nothing to do with the age, the strumpet, or Tom.

Paine himself, never known for his modesty, stated the matter much more simply, as reported by his friend Benjamin Rush: "He said he was at a loss to know whether he was made for the times, or the times made for him."

If Adams gave vent to his spleen as well as to his intellectual convictions, his earlier "pulling down" remark might have well been applied to the age in which Paine lived. Enlightened thinkers in England, Europe, and America were cutting through encrusted institutions inherited from the past. It was a demolition culminating in what a recent historian has called "The Age of the Democratic Revolution," of which America's was the grand beginning.

Such was Paine's vision; it is the vision with which *Common Sense* is permeated. And for a moment, America caught that vision as Paine's searing prose turned thirteen dissonant rebellions into a revolution. By this measure, *Common Sense*, along with the Declaration and the Constitution, is one of the fundamental testaments of the American Republic, and Paine, with Franklin and Jefferson, is one of the progenitors of American democracy.

COMMON SENSE;

ADDRESSED TO THE

INHABITANTS

OF

AMERICA,

On the following interesting

SUBJECTS:

I. Of the Origin and Design of Government in general, with concise Remarks on the English Constitution.

II. Of Monarchy and Hereditary Succession.

III. Thoughts on the present State of American Affairs.

IV. Of the present ability of America, with some miscellaneous Reflections.

A NEW EDITION, with several Additions in the Body of the Work. To which is Added an APPENDIX; together with an Address to the People called QUAKERS.

Man knows no Master save creating HEAVEN,
Or those whom choice and common Good ordain.
THOMSON.

PHILADELPHIA:

PRINTED and SOLD by W. and T. BRADFORD.

M,DCC,LXXVI.

[PRICE ONE BRITISH SHILLING.]

IN THE CAUSE OF
LIBERTY
AND
My COUNTRY
the 1781
Common Sense

C.W. Peale Pinx. Philadelphia   James Watson Fecit

COMMON SENSE
INTRODUCTION[1]

PERHAPS the sentiments contained in the following pages, are not *yet* sufficiently fashionable to procure them general favor; a long habit of not thinking a thing *wrong*, gives it a superficial appearance of being *right*, and raises at first a formidable outcry in defence of custom. But the tumult soon subsides. Time makes more converts than reason.

As a long and violent abuse of power, is generally the Means of calling the right of it in question (and in Matters too which might never have been thought of, had not the Sufferers been aggravated into the inquiry) and as the King of England hath undertaken in his *own Right*, to support the Parliament in what he calls *Theirs*, and as the good people of this country are grievously oppressed by the combination, they have an undoubted privilege to inquire into the pretensions of both, and equally to reject the usurpation of either.

In the following sheets, the author hath studiously avoided every thing which is personal among ourselves. Compliments as well as censure to individuals make no part thereof. The wise, and the worthy, need not the triumph of a pamphlet; and those whose sentiments are injudicious, or unfriendly, will cease of themselves unless too much pains are bestowed upon their conversion.

The cause of America is in a great measure the cause of all mankind. Many circumstances hath, and will arise, which are not local, but universal, and through which the principles of all Lovers of Mankind are affected, and in the Event of which, their Affections are interested. The laying a Country desolate with Fire and Sword, declaring War against the natural rights of all Mankind, and extirpating the Defenders thereof from the Face of the Earth, is the Concern of every Man to whom Nature hath given the Power of feeling; of which Class, regardless of Party Censure, is the

AUTHOR.

P.S. The Publication of this new Edition hath been delayed, with a View of taking notice (had it been necessary) of any Attempt to refute the Doctrine of Independence: As no Answer hath yet appeared, it is now presumed that none will, the Time needful for getting such a Performance ready for the Public being considerably past.[2]

Who the Author of this Production is, is wholly unnecessary to the Public, as the Object for Attention is the *Doctrine itself*, not the *Man*. Yet it may not be unnecessary to say, That he is unconnected with any Party, and under no sort of Influence public or private, but the influence of reason and principle.

Philadelphia, February 14, 1776

Of the origin and design of government in general.
With concise remarks on the English constitution

Some writers have so confounded society with government, as to leave little or no distinction between them; whereas they are not only different, but have different origins. Society is produced by our wants, and government by our wickedness; the former promotes our happiness *positively* by uniting our affections, the latter *negatively* by restraining our vices. The one encourages intercourse, the other creates distinctions. The first is a patron, the last a punisher.

Society in every state is a blessing, but government even in its best state is but a necessary evil; [3] in its worst state an intolerable one; for when we suffer, or are exposed to the same miseries *by a government*, which we might expect in a country *without government*, our calamity is heightened by reflecting that we furnish the means by which we suffer. Government, like dress, is the badge of lost innocence; the palaces of kings are built on the ruins of the bowers of paradise. For were the impulses of conscience clear, uniform, and irresistibly obeyed, man would need no other lawgiver; but that not being the case, he finds it necessary to surrender up a part of his property to furnish means for the protection of the rest; and this he is induced to do by the same prudence which in every other case advises him out of two evils to choose the least. *Wherefore*, security being the true design and end of government, it unanswerably follows, that whatever *form* thereof appears most likely to ensure it to us, with the least expence and greatest benefit, is preferable to all others.[4]

In order to gain a clear and just idea of the design and end of government, let us suppose a small number of persons settled in some sequestered part of the earth, unconnected with the rest, they will then represent the first peopling of any country, or of the world. In this state of natural liberty, society will be their first thought. A thousand motives will excite them thereto, the strength of one man is so unequal to his wants, and his mind so unfitted for perpetual solitude, that he is soon obliged to seek assistance and relief of another, who in his turn requires the same. Four or five united would be able to raise a tolerable dwelling in the midst of a wilderness, but *one* man might labour out the common period of life without accomplishing any thing; when he had felled his timber he could not remove it, nor erect it after it was removed; hunger in the mean time would urge him from his work, and every different want call him a different way. Disease, nay even misfortune would be death, for though neither might be mortal, yet either would disable him from living, and reduce him to a state in which he might rather be said to perish than to die.

Thus necessity, like a gravitating power,[5] would soon form our newly arrived emigrants into society, the reciprocal blessings of which, would supersede, and render the obligations of law and government unnecessary while they remained perfectly just to each other; but as nothing but heaven is impregnable to vice, it will unavoidably happen, that in proportion as they surmount the first difficulties of emigration, which bound them together in a common cause, they will begin to relax in their duty and attachment to each other; and this remissness will point out the necessity of establishing some form of government to supply the defect of moral virtue.

Some convenient tree will afford them a State-House, under the branches of which, the whole colony may assemble to deliberate on public matters. It is more than probable that their first laws will have the title only of REGULATIONS, and be enforced by no other penalty than public disesteem. In this first parliament every man, by natural right, will have a seat.

But as the colony increases, the public concerns will increase likewise, and the distance at which the members may be separated, will render it too inconvenient for all of them to meet on every occasion as at first, when their number was small, their habitations near, and the public concerns few and trifling. This will point out the convenience of their consenting to leave the legislative part to be managed by a select number chosen from the whole body, who are supposed to have the same concerns at stake which those have who appointed them, and who will act in the same manner as the whole body would act, were they present. If the colony continue increasing, it will become necessary to augment the number of the representatives, and that the interest of every part of the colony may be attended to, it will be found best to divide the whole into convenient parts, each part sending its proper number; and that the *elected* might never form to themselves an interest separate from the *electors*, prudence will point out the propriety of having elections often; because as the *elected* might by that means return and mix again with the general body of the *elec-*

tors in a few months, their fidelity to the public will be secured by the prudent reflexion of not making a rod for themselves. And as this frequent interchange will establish a common interest with every part of the community, they will mutually and naturally support each other, and on this (not on the unmeaning name of king) depends the *strength of government, and the happiness of the governed*.

Here then is the origin and rise of government; namely, a mode rendered necessary by the inability of moral virtue to govern the world; here too is the design and end of government, viz. freedom and security. And however our eyes may be dazzled with show, or our ears deceived by sound; however prejudice may warp our wills, or interest darken our understanding, the simple voice of nature and of reason will say, it is right.

I draw my idea of the form of government from a principle in nature, which no art can overturn, viz. that the more simple any thing is, the less liable it is to be disordered, and the easier repaired when disordered; and with this maxim in view, I offer a few remarks on the so much boasted constitution of England. That it was noble for the dark and slavish times in which it was erected, is granted. When the world was overrun with tyranny the least remove therefrom was a glorious rescue. But that it is imperfect, subject to convulsions, and incapable of producing what it seems to promise, is easily demonstrated.

Absolute governments (tho' the disgrace of human nature) have this advantage with them, that they are simple; if the people suffer, they know the head from which their suffering springs, know likewise the remedy, and are not bewildered by a variety of causes and cures. But the constitution of England is so exceedingly complex, that the nation may suffer for years together without being able to discover in which part the fault lies; some will say in one and some in another, and every political physician will advise a different medicine.

I know it is difficult to get over local or long standing prejudices, yet if we will suffer ourselves to examine the component parts of the English constitution, we shall find them to be the base remains of two ancient tyrannies, compounded with some new republican materials.

First.—The remains of monarchical tyranny in the person of the king.

Secondly.—The remains of aristocratical tyranny in the persons of the peers.

Thirdly.—The new republican materials in the persons of the commons, on whose virtue depends the freedom of England.

The two first, by being hereditary, are independent of the people; wherefore in a *constitutional sense* they contribute nothing towards the freedom of the state.

To say that the constitution of England is a *union* of three powers reciprocally *checking* each other, is farcical, either the words have no meaning, or they are flat contradictions.

To say that the commons is a check upon the king, presupposes two things:

First.—That the king is not to be trusted without being looked after, or in other words, that a thirst for absolute power is the natural disease of monarchy.

Secondly.—That the commons, by being appointed for that purpose, are either wiser or more worthy of confidence than the crown.

But as the same constitution which gives the commons a power to check the king by withholding the supplies, gives afterwards the king a power to check the commons, by empowering him to reject their other bills; it again supposes that the king is wiser than those whom it has already supposed to be wiser than him. A mere absurdity!

There is something exceedingly ridiculous in the composition of monarchy; it first excludes a man from the means of information, yet empowers him to act in cases where the highest judgment is required. The state of a king shuts him from the world, yet the business of a king requires him to know it thoroughly; wherefore the different parts, by unnaturally opposing and destroying each other, prove the whole character to be absurd and useless.

Some writers have explained the English constitution thus: The king, say they, is one, the people another; the peers are an house in behalf of the king, the commons in behalf of the people; but this hath all the distinctions of an house divided against itself; [6] and though the expressions be pleasantly arranged, yet when examined, they appear idle and ambiguous; and it will always happen, that the nicest construction that words are capable of, when applied to the description of some thing which either cannot exist, or is too incomprehensible to be within the compass of description, will be words of sound only, and though they may amuse the ear, they cannot inform the mind, for this explanation includes a previous question, viz. *How came the king by a power which the people are afraid to trust, and always obliged to check?* Such a power could not be the gift of a wise people, neither can any power, *which needs checking,* be from God; yet the provision, which the constitution makes, supposes such a power to exist.

But the provision is unequal to the task; the means either cannot or will not accomplish the end, and the whole affair is a felo de se; [7] for as the greater weight will always carry up the less, and as all the wheels of a machine are put in motion by one, it only remains to know which power in the constitution has the most weight, for that will govern; and though the others, or a part of them, may clog, or, as the phrase is, check the rapidity of its motion, yet so long as they cannot stop it, their endeavours will be ineffectual; the first moving power will at last have its way, and what it wants in speed, is supplied by time.

That the crown is this overbearing part in the English constitution, needs not be mentioned, and that it derives its whole consequence merely from being the giver of places and pensions, is self-evident, wherefore, though we have been wise enough to shut and lock a door against absolute monarchy, we at the same time have been foolish enough to put the crown in possession of the key.

The prejudice of Englishmen in favour of their own government by king, lords and commons, arises as much or more from national pride than reason. Individuals are undoubtedly safer in England than in some other countries, but the *will* of the king is as much the *law* of the land in Britain as in France, with this difference, that instead of proceeding directly from his mouth, it is handed to the people under the more formidable shape of an act of parliament. For the fate of Charles the First hath only made kings more subtle—not more just.[8]

Wherefore, laying aside all national pride and prejudice in favour of modes and forms, the plain truth is, that *it is wholly owing to the constitution of the people, and not to the constitution of the government*, that the crown is not as oppressive in England as in Turkey.

An inquiry into the *constitutional errors* in the English form of government is at this time highly necessary; for as we are never in a proper condition of doing justice to others, while we continue under the influence of some leading partiality, so neither are we capable of doing it to ourselves while we remain fettered by any obstinate prejudice. And as a man, who is attached to a prostitute, is unfitted to choose or judge a wife, so any prepossession in favour of a rotten constitution of government will disable us from discerning a good one.

Of monarchy and hereditary succession

Mankind being originally equals in the order of creation, the equality could only be destroyed by some subsequent circumstance; the distinctions of rich, and poor, may in a great measure be accounted for, and that without having recourse to the harsh, ill-sounding names of oppression and avarice.[9] Oppression is often the *consequence*, but seldom or never the *means* of riches; and though avarice will preserve a man from being necessitously poor, it generally makes him too timorous to be wealthy.

But there is another and greater distinction, for which no truly natural or religious reason can be assigned, and that is, the distinction of men into KINGS and SUBJECTS. Male and female are the distinctions of nature, good and bad the distinctions of heaven; but how a race of men came into the world so exalted above the rest, and distinguished like some new species, is worth inquiring into, and whether they are the means of happiness or of misery to mankind.

In the early ages of the world, according to the scripture chronology, there were no kings; the consequence of which was, there were no wars; it is the pride of kings which throw mankind into confusion. Holland without a king hath enjoyed more peace for this last century than any of the monarchical governments in Europe.[10] Antiquity favours the same remark; for the quiet and rural lives of the first patriarchs hath a happy something in them, which vanishes away when we come to the history of Jewish royalty.

Government by kings was first introduced into the world by the Heathens, from whom the children of Israel copied the custom. It was the most prosperous invention the Devil ever set on foot for the promotion of idolatry. The Heathens paid divine honors to their deceased kings, and the Christian world hath improved on the plan, by doing the same to their living ones. How impious is the title of sacred majesty applied to a worm, who in the midst of his splendor is crumbling into dust!

As the exalting one man so greatly above the rest cannot be justified on the equal rights of nature, so neither can it be defended on the authority of scripture; for the will of the Almighty, as declared by Gideon and the prophet Samuel, expressly disapproves of government by kings.[11] All antimonarchical parts of scripture have been very smoothly glossed over in monarchical governments, but they undoubtedly merit the attention of countries which have their governments yet to form. *"Render unto Cæsar the things which are Cæsar's"* is the scripture doctrine of courts, yet it is no support of monarchical government, for the Jews at that time were without a king, and in a state of vassalage to the Romans.

Near three thousand years passed away from the Mosaic account of the creation, till the Jews under a national delusion requested a king. Till then their form of government (except in extraordinary cases, where the Almighty interposed) was a kind of republic administered by a judge and the elders of the tribes. Kings they had none, and it was held sinful to acknowledge any being under that title but the Lord of Hosts. And when a man seriously reflects on the idolatrous homage which is paid to the persons of kings, he need not wonder that the Almighty, ever jealous of his honor, should disapprove of a form of government which so impiously invades the prerogative of heaven.

Monarchy is ranked in scripture as one of the sins of the Jews, for which a curse in reserve is denounced against them. The history of that transaction is worth attending to.

The children of Israel being oppressed by the Midianites, Gideon marched against them with a small army, and victory, thro' the divine interposition, decided in his favour. The Jews, elate with success, and attributing it to the generalship of Gideon, proposed making him a king, saying, *Rule thou over us, thou and thy son and thy son's son.* Here was temptation in its fullest extent; not a kingdom only, but an hereditary one, but Gideon in the piety of his soul replied, *I will not rule over you, neither shall my son rule over you,* THE LORD SHALL RULE OVER YOU. Words need not be more explicit; Gideon doth not decline the honor, but denieth their right to give it; neither doth he compliment them with invented declarations of his thanks, but in the positive stile of a prophet charges them with disaffection to their proper Sovereign, the King of heaven.

About one hundred and thirty years after this, they fell again into the same error. The hankering which the Jews had for the idolatrous customs of the Heathens, is something exceedingly unaccountable; but so it was, that laying hold of the misconduct of Samuel's two sons, who were

entrusted with some secular concerns, they came
in an abrupt and clamorous manner to Samuel,
saying, *Behold thou art old, and thy sons walk
not in thy ways, now make us a king to judge us,
like all the other nations.* And here we cannot but
observe that their motives were bad, viz. that they
might be *like* unto other nations, i. e. the Heathens, whereas their true glory laid in being as
much *unlike* them as possible. *But the thing dis-
pleased Samuel when they said, Give us a king to
judge us; and Samuel prayed unto the Lord, and
the Lord said unto Samuel, Hearken unto the
voice of the people in all that they say unto thee,
for they have not rejected thee, but they have rejected me,* THAT I SHOULD NOT REIGN OVER
THEM. *According to all the works which they have
done since the day that I brought them up out of
Egypt, even unto this day; wherewith they have
forsaken me and served other Gods; so do they
also unto thee. Now therefore hearken unto their
voice, howbeit, protest solemnly unto them and
shew them the manner of the king that shall reign
over them, i.e.* not of any particular king, but the
general manner of the kings of the earth, whom
Israel was so eagerly copying after. And notwithstanding the great distance of time and difference
of manners, the character is still in fashion. *And
Samuel told all the words of the Lord unto the
people, that asked of him a king. And he said,
This shall be the manner of the king that shall*

reign over you; he will take your sons and appoint them for himself, for his chariots, and to be his horsemen, and some shall run before his chariots (this description agrees with the present mode of impressing men) *and he will appoint him captains over thousands and captains over fifties, and will set them to ear his ground and to reap his harvest, and to make his instruments of war, and instruments of his chariots; and he will take your daughters to be confectionaries, and to be cooks and to be bakers* (this describes the expence and luxury as well as the oppression of kings) *and he will take your fields and your olive yards, even the best of them, and give them to his servants; and he will take the tenth of your seed, and of your vineyards, and give them to his officers and to his servants* (by which we see that bribery, corruption and favouritism are the standing vices of kings) *and he will take the tenth of your men servants, and your maid servants, and your goodliest young men and your asses, and put them to his work; and he will take the tenth of your sheep, and ye shall be his servants, and ye shall cry out in that day because of your king which ye shall have chosen,* AND THE LORD WILL NOT HEAR YOU IN THAT DAY. This accounts for the continuation of monarchy; neither do the characters of the few good kings which have lived since, either sanctify the title, or blot out the sinfulness of the origin; the high encomium given of David takes no notice of him *officially as a king*, but only as a *man* after God's own heart. *Nevertheless the people refused to obey the voice of Samuel, and they said, Nay, but we will have a king over us, that we may be like all the nations, and that our king may judge us, and go out before us, and fight our battles.* Samuel continued to reason with them, but to no purpose; he set before them their ingratitude, but all would not avail; and seeing them fully bent on their folly, he cried out, *I will call unto the Lord, and he shall send thunder and rain* (which then was a punishment, being in the time of wheat harvest) *that ye may perceive and see that your wickedness is great which ye have done in the sight of the Lord,* IN ASKING YOU A KING. *So Samuel called unto the Lord, and the Lord sent thunder and rain that day, and all the people greatly feared the Lord and Samuel. And all the people said unto Samuel, pray for thy servants unto the Lord thy God that we die not, for* WE HAVE ADDED UNTO OUR SINS THIS EVIL, TO ASK A KING. These portions of scripture are direct and positive. They admit of no equivocal construction. That the Almighty hath here entered his protest against monarchical government, is true, or the scripture is false. And a man hath good reason to believe that there is as much of king-craft, as priest-craft, in withholding the scripture from the public in Popish countries. For monarchy in every instance is the Popery of government.[12]

To the evil of monarchy we have added that of hereditary succession; and as the first is a degradation and lessening of ourselves, so the second, claimed as a matter of right, is an insult and an imposition on posterity. For all men being originally equals, no *one* by *birth* could have a right to set up his own family in perpetual preference to all others for ever, and though himself might deserve *some* decent degree of honors of his cotemporaries, yet his descendants might be far too unworthy to inherit them. One of the strongest *natural* proofs of the folly of hereditary right in kings, is, that nature disapproves it, otherwise she would not so frequently turn it into ridicule by giving mankind an *Ass for a Lion.*

Secondly, as no man at first could possess any other public honors than were bestowed upon him, so the givers of those honors could have no power to give away the right of posterity. And though they might say, "We choose you for *our* head," they could not, without manifest injustice to their children, say "that your children and your childrens children shall reign over *ours* for ever." Because such an unwise, unjust, unnatural compact might (perhaps) in the next succession put them under the government of a rogue or a fool. Most wise men, in their private sentiments, have ever treated hereditary right with contempt; yet it is one of those evils, which when once established is not easily removed; many submit from fear, others from superstition, and the more powerful part shares with the king the plunder of the rest.

This is supposing the present race of kings in the world to have had an honorable origin; whereas it is more than probable, that could we take off the dark covering of antiquity, and trace them to their first rise, that we should find the first of them nothing better than the principal ruffian of some restless gang, whose savage manners or pre-eminence in subtilty obtained him the title of chief among plunderers; and who by increasing in power, and extending his depredations, overawed the quiet and defenceless to purchase their safety by frequent contributions. Yet his electors could have no idea of giving hereditary right to his descendants, because such a perpetual exclusion of themselves was incompatible with the free and unrestrained principles they professed to live by. Wherefore, hereditary succession in the early ages of monarchy could not take place as a matter of claim, but as something casual or complimental; but as few or no records were extant in those days, and traditionary history stuffed with fables, it was very easy, after the lapse of a few generations, to trump up some superstitious tale, conveniently timed, Mahomet like, to cram hereditary right down the throats of the vulgar.[13] Perhaps the disorders which threatened, or seemed to threaten, on the decease of a leader and the choice of a new one (for elections among ruffians could not be very orderly) induced many at first to favor hereditary pretensions; by which means it happened, as it hath happened since, that what at first was submitted to as a convenience, was afterwards claimed as a right.

England, since the conquest, hath known some few good monarchs, but groaned beneath a much larger number of bad ones; yet no man in his senses can say that their claim under William the Conqueror is a very honorable one.[14] A French bastard landing with an armed banditti, and establishing himself king of England against the consent of the natives, is in plain terms a very paltry rascally original.—It certainly hath no divinity in it. However, it is needless to spend much time in exposing the folly of hereditary right; if there are any so weak as to believe it, let them promiscuously worship the ass and lion, and welcome. I shall neither copy their humility, nor disturb their devotion.

Yet I should be glad to ask how they suppose kings came at first? The question admits but of three answers, viz. either by lot, by election, or by usurpation. If the first king was taken by lot, it establishes a precedent for the next, which excludes hereditary succession. Saul was by lot, yet the succession was not hereditary, neither does it appear from that transaction there was any intention it ever should.[15] If the first king of any country was by election, that likewise establishes a precedent for the next; for to say, that the *right* of all future generations is taken away, by the act of the first electors, in their choice not only of a king, but of a family of kings for ever, hath no parallel in or out of scripture but the doctrine of original sin, which supposes the free will of all men lost in Adam; and from such comparison, and it will admit of no other, hereditary succession can derive no glory. For as in Adam all sinned, and as in the first electors all men obeyed; as in the one all mankind were subjected to Satan, and in the other to Sovereignty; as our innocence was lost in the first, and our authority in the last; and as both disable us from reassuming some former state and privilege, it unanswerably follows that original sin and hereditary succession are parallels. Dishonorable rank! Inglorious connexion! Yet the most subtile sophist cannot produce a juster simile.

As to usurpation, no man will be so hardy as to defend it; and that William the Conqueror was an usurper is a fact not to be contradicted. The plain truth is, that the antiquity of English monarchy will not bear looking into.

But it is not so much the absurdity as the evil of hereditary succession which concerns mankind. Did it ensure a race of good and wise men it would have the seal of divine authority, but as it opens a door to the *foolish*, the *wicked*, and the *improper*, it hath in it the nature of oppression. Men who look upon themselves born to reign, and others to obey, soon grow insolent; selected from the rest of mankind their minds are early poisoned by importance; and the world they act in differs so materially from the world at large, that they have but little opportunity of knowing its true interests, and when they succeed to the government are frequently the most ignorant and unfit of any throughout the dominions.

Another evil which attends hereditary succession is, that the throne is subject to be possessed by a minor at any age; all which time the regency, acting under the cover of a king, have every opportunity and inducement to betray their trust. The same national misfortune happens, when a king, worn out with age and infirmity, enters the last stage of human weakness. In both these cases the public becomes a prey to every miscreant, who can tamper successfully with the follies either of age or infancy.

The most plausible plea, which hath ever been offered in favour of hereditary succession, is, that it preserves a nation from civil wars; and were this true, it would be weighty; whereas, it is the most barefaced falsity ever imposed upon mankind. The whole history of England disowns the fact. Thirty kings and two minors have reigned in that distracted kingdom since the conquest, in which time there have been (including the Revolution) no less than eight civil wars and nineteen rebellions. Wherefore instead of making for peace, it makes against it, and destroys the very foundation it seems to stand on.

The contest for monarchy and succession, between the houses of York and Lancaster, laid England in a scene of blood for many years. Twelve pitched battles, besides skirmishes and sieges, were fought between Henry and Edward. Twice was Henry prisoner to Edward, who in his turn was prisoner to Henry. And so uncertain is the fate of war and the temper of a nation, when nothing but personal matters are the ground of a quarrel, that Henry was taken in triumph from a prison to a palace, and Edward obliged to fly from a palace to a foreign land; yet, as sudden transitions of temper are seldom lasting, Henry in his turn was driven from the throne, and Edward recalled to succeed him. The parliament always following the strongest side.

This contest began in the reign of Henry the Sixth, and was not entirely extinguished till Henry the Seventh, in whom the families were united. Including a period of 67 years, viz. from 1422 to 1489.[16]

In short, monarchy and succession have laid (not this or that kingdom only) but the world in blood and ashes. 'Tis a form of government which the word of God bears testimony against, and blood will attend it.

If we inquire into the business of a king, we shall find that in some countries they have none; and after sauntering away their lives without pleasure to themselves or advantage to the nation, withdraw from the scene, and leave their successors to tread the same idle ground. In absolute monarchies the whole weight of business, civil and military, lies on the king; the children of Israel in their request for a king, urged this plea "that he may judge us, and go out before us and fight our battles." But in countries where he is neither a judge nor a general, as in England, a man would be puzzled to know what *is* his business.

The nearer any government approaches to a republic the less business there is for a king. It is somewhat difficult to find a proper name for the government of England. Sir William Meredith calls it a republic;[17] but in its present state it is unworthy of the name, because the corrupt influence of the crown, by having all the places in its disposal, hath so effectually swallowed up the power, and eaten out the virtue of the house of commons (the republican part in the constitution) that the government of England is nearly as monarchical as that of France or Spain. Men fall out with names without understanding them. For it is the republican and not the monarchical part of the constitution of England which Englishmen glory in, viz. the liberty of choosing an house of commons from out of their own body—and it is easy to see that when republican virtue fails, slavery ensues. Why is the constitution of England sickly, but because monarchy hath poisoned the republic, the crown hath engrossed the commons?

In England a king hath little more to do than to make war and give away places; which in plain terms, is to impoverish the nation and set it together by the ears. A pretty business indeed for a man to be allowed eight hundred thousand sterling a year for, and worshipped into the bargain! Of more worth is one honest man to society and in the sight of God, than all the crowned ruffians that ever lived.

Thoughts on the present state of American affairs

In the following pages I offer nothing more than simple facts, plain arguments, and common sense; and have no other preliminaries to settle with the reader, than that he will divest himself of prejudice and prepossession, and suffer his reason and his feelings to determine for themselves; that he will put *on*, or rather that he will not put *off* the true character of a man, and generously enlarge his views beyond the present day.

Volumes have been written on the subject of the struggle between England and America. Men of all ranks have embarked in the controversy, from different motives, and with various designs; but all have been ineffectual, and the period of debate is closed. Arms, as the last resource, decide the contest; the appeal was the choice of the king, and the continent hath accepted the challenge.

It hath been reported of the late Mr. Pelham (who tho' an able minister was not without his faults) that on his being attacked in the house of commons, on the score, that his measures were only of a temporary kind, replied *"they will last my time."* [18] Should a thought so fatal and unmanly possess the colonies in the present contest, the name of ancestors will be remembered by future generations with detestation.

The sun never shined on a cause of greater worth. 'Tis not the affair of a city, a county, a province, or a kingdom, but of a continent—of at least one eighth part of the habitable globe. 'Tis not the concern of a day, a year, or an age; posterity are virtually involved in the contest, and will be more or less affected, even to the end of time, by the proceedings now. Now is the seed-time of continental union, faith and honor. The least fracture now will be like a name engraved with the point of a pin on the tender rind of a young oak; the wound will enlarge with the tree, and posterity read it in full grown characters.

By referring the matter from argument to arms, a new æra for politics is struck; a new method of thinking hath arisen. All plans, proposals, &c. prior to the nineteenth of April, *i. e.* to the commencement of hostilities, are like the almanacks of the last year; which, though proper then are superseded and useless now. Whatever was advanced by the advocates on either side of the question then, terminated in one and the same point, viz. a union with Great-Britain; the only difference between the parties was the method of effecting it; the one proposing force, the other friendship; but it hath so far happened that the first hath failed, and the second hath withdrawn her influence.

As much hath been said of the advantages of reconciliation, which, like an agreeable dream, hath passed away and left us as we were, it is but right, that we should examine the contrary side of the argument, and inquire into some of the many material injuries which these colonies sustain, and always will sustain, by being connected with, and dependant on Great-Britain: To examine that connexion and dependance, on the principles of nature and common sense, to see what we have to trust to, if separated, and what we are to expect, if dependant.

I have heard it asserted by some, that as America hath flourished under her former connexion with Great-Britain, that the same connexion is necessary towards her future happiness, and will always have the same effect. Nothing can be more fallacious than this kind of argument. We may as well assert that because a child has thrived upon milk, that it is never to have meat, or that the first twenty years of our lives is to become a precedent for the next twenty. But even this is admitting more than is true, for I answer roundly, that America would have flourished as much, and probably much more, had no European power had any thing to do with her. The commerce, by which she hath enriched herself, are the necessaries of life, and will always have a market while eating is the custom of Europe.

But she has protected us, say some. That she has engrossed us is true, and defended the continent at our expense as well as her own is admitted, and she would have defended Turkey from the same motive, viz. the sake of trade and dominion.

Alas, we have been long led away by ancient prejudices, and made large sacrifices to superstition. We have boasted the protection of Great-Britain, without considering, that her motive was *interest* not *attachment;* that she did not protect us from *our enemies* on *our account,* but from *her enemies* on *her own account,* from those who had no quarrel with us on any *other account,* and who will always be our enemies on the *same account.* Let Britain wave her pretensions to the continent, or the continent throw off the dependance, and we should be at peace with France and Spain were they at war with Britain. The miseries of Hanover last war ought to warn us against connexions.[19]

It has lately been asserted in parliament, that the colonies have no relation to each other but through the parent country, *i. e.* that Pennsylvania and the Jerseys, and so on for the rest, are sister colonies by the way of England; this is certainly a very round-about way of proving relationship, but it is the nearest and only true way of proving enemyship, if I may so call it. France and Spain never were, nor perhaps ever will be our enemies as *Americans,* but as our being the *subjects of Great-Britain.*

But Britain is the parent country, say some. Then the more shame upon her conduct. Even brutes do not devour their young, nor savages make war upon their families; wherefore the assertion, if true, turns to her reproach; but it happens not to be true, or only partly so, and the phrase *parent* or *mother country* hath been jesuitically adopted by the king and his parasites, with a low papistical design of gaining an unfair bias on the credulous weakness of our minds. Europe, and not England, is the parent country of America. This new world hath been the asylum for the persecuted lovers of civil and religious liberty from *every part* of Europe. Hither have they fled, not from the tender embraces of the mother, but from the cruelty of the monster; and it is so far true of England, that the same tyranny which drove the first emigrants from home, pursues their descendants still.

In this extensive quarter of the globe, we forget the narrow limits of three hundred and sixty miles (the extent of England) and carry our friendship on a larger scale; we claim brotherhood with every European Christian, and triumph in the generosity of the sentiment.

It is pleasant to observe by what regular gradations we surmount the force of local prejudice, as we enlarge our acquaintance with the world. A man born in any town in England divided into parishes, will naturally associate most with his fellow-parishioners (because their interests in many cases will be common) and distinguish him by the name of *neighbour;* if he meet him but a few miles from home, he drops the narrow idea of a street, and salutes him by the name of *townsman;* if he travel out of the county, and meet him in any other, he forgets the minor divisions of street and town, and calls him *countryman,* i. e. *countyman;* but if in their foreign excursions they should associate in France or any other part of *Europe,* their local remembrance would be enlarged into that of *Englishmen*. And by a just parity of reasoning, all Europeans meeting in America, or any other quarter of the globe, are *countrymen*; for England, Holland, Germany, or Sweden, when compared with the whole, stand in the same places on the larger scale, which the divisions of street, town, and county do on the smaller ones; distinctions too limited for continental minds. Not one third of the inhabitants, even of this province, are of English descent.[20] Wherefore I reprobate the phrase of parent or mother country applied to England only, as being false, selfish, narrow and ungenerous.

But admitting, that we were all of English descent, what does it amount to? Nothing. Britain, being now an open enemy, extinguishes every other name and title: And to say that reconciliation is our duty, is truly farcical. The first king of England, of the present line (William the Conqueror) was a Frenchman, and half the Peers of England are descendants from the same country; wherefore, by the same method of reasoning, England ought to be governed by France.[21]

Much hath been said of the united strength of Britain and the colonies, that in conjunction they might bid defiance to the world. But this is mere presumption; the fate of war is uncertain, neither do the expressions mean any thing; for this

continent would never suffer itself to be drained
of inhabitants, to support the British arms in
either Asia, Africa, or Europe.

Besides what have we to do with setting the
world at defiance? Our plan is commerce, and
that, well attended to, will secure us the peace
and friendship of all Europe; because, it is the
interest of all Europe to have America a *free port*.
Her trade will always be a protection, and her
barrenness of gold and silver secure her from in-
vaders.

I challenge the warmest advocate for reconciliation, to shew, a single advantage that this
continent can reap, by being connected with Great-
Britain. I repeat the challenge, not a single advantage is derived. Our corn will fetch its price
in any market in Europe, and our imported goods
must be paid for buy them where we will.

But the injuries and disadvantages we sustain
by that connection, are without number; and our
duty to mankind at large, as well as to ourselves,
instruct us to renounce the alliance: Because, any
submission to, or dependance on Great-Britain,
tends directly to involve this continent in European wars and quarrels; and sets us at variance
with nations, who would otherwise seek our
friendship, and against whom, we have neither

anger nor complaint. As Europe is our market for trade, we ought to form no partial connection with any part of it. It is the true interest of America to steer clear of European contentions,[22] which she never can do, while by her dependance on Britain, she is made the make-weight in the scale of British politics.

Europe is too thickly planted with kingdoms to be long at peace, and whenever a war breaks out between England and any foreign power, the trade of America goes to ruin, *because of her connection with Britain*. The next war may not turn out like the last, and should it not, the advocates for reconciliation now, will be wishing for separation then, because, neutrality in that case, would be a safer convoy than a man of war. Every thing that is right or natural pleads for separation. The blood of the slain, the weeping voice of nature cries, 'TIS TIME TO PART. Even the distance at which the Almighty hath placed England and America, is a strong and natural proof, that the authority of the one, over the other, was never the design of Heaven. The time likewise at which the continent was discovered, adds weight to the argument, and the manner in which it was peopled encreases the force of it. The reformation was preceded by the discovery of America, as if the Almighty graciously meant to open a sanctuary to the persecuted in future years, when home should afford neither friendship nor safety.[23]

The authority of Great-Britain over this continent, is a form of government, which sooner or later must have an end: And a serious mind can draw no true pleasure by looking forward, under the painful and positive conviction, that what he calls "the present constitution" is merely temporary. As parents, we can have no joy, knowing that *this government* is not sufficiently lasting to ensure any thing which we may bequeath to posterity: And by a plain method of argument, as we are running the next generation into debt, we ought to do the work of it, otherwise we use them meanly and pitifully. In order to discover the line of our duty rightly, we should take our children in our hand, and fix our station a few years farther into life; that eminence will present a prospect, which a few present fears and prejudices conceal from our sight.

Though I would carefully avoid giving unnecessary offence, yet I am inclined to believe, that all those who espouse the doctrine of reconciliation, may be included within the following descriptions. Interested men, who are not to be trusted; weak men, who *cannot* see; prejudiced men, who *will not* see; and a certain set of moderate men, who think better of the European world than it deserves; and this last class, by an ill-judged deliberation, will be the cause of more calamities to this continent, than all the other three.

It is the good fortune of many to live distant from the scene of sorrow; the evil is not sufficient brought to *their* doors to make *them* feel the precariousness with which all American property is possessed. But let our imaginations transport us for a few moments to Boston, that seat of wretchedness will teach us wisdom, and instruct us for ever to renounce a power in whom we can have no trust. The inhabitants of that unfortunate city, who but a few months ago were in ease and affluence, have now, no other alternative than to stay and starve, or turn out to beg. Endangered by the fire of their friends if they continue within the city, and plundered by the soldiery if they leave it. In their present condition they are prisoners without the hope of redemption, and in a general attack for their relief, they would be exposed to the fury of both armies.

Men of passive tempers look somewhat lightly over the offences of Britain, and, still hoping for the best, are apt to call out, *"Come, come, we shall be friends again, for all this."* But examine the passions and feelings of mankind, Bring the doctrine of reconciliation to the touchstone of nature, and then tell me, whether you can hereafter love, honor, and faithfully serve the power that hath carried fire and sword into your land? If you cannot do all these, then are you only deceiving yourselves, and by your delay bringing ruin upon posterity. Your future connexion with Britain, whom you can neither love nor honor, will be forced and unnatural, and being formed only on the plan of present convenience, will in a little time fall into a relapse more wretched than the first. But if you say, you can still pass the violations over, then I ask, Hath your house been burnt? Hath your property been destroyed before your face? Are your wife and children destitute of a bed to lie on, or bread to live on? Have you lost a parent or a child by their hands, and yourself the ruined and wretched survivor? If you have not, then are you not a judge of those who have. But if you have, and still can shake hands with the murderers, then are you unworthy the name of husband, father, friend, or lover, and whatever may be your rank or title in life, you have the heart of a coward, and the spirit of a sycophant.

This is not inflaming or exaggerating matters, but trying them by those feelings and affections which nature justifies, and without which, we should be incapable of discharging the social duties of life, or enjoying the felicities of it. I mean not to exhibit horror for the purpose of provoking revenge, but to awaken us from fatal and unmanly slumbers, that we may pursue determinately some fixed object. It is not in the power of Britain or of Europe to conquer America, if she do not conquer herself by *delay* and *timidity*. The present winter is worth an age if rightly employed, but if lost or neglected, the whole continent will partake of the misfortune; and there is no punishment which that man will not deserve, be he who, or what, or where he will, that may be the means of sacrificing a season so precious and useful.

It is repugnant to reason, to the universal order of things, to all examples from former ages, to suppose, that this continent can longer remain subject to any external power. The most sanguine in Britain does not think so. The utmost stretch of human wisdom cannot, at this time, compass a plan short of separation, which can promise the continent even a year's security. Reconciliation is *now* a fallacious dream. Nature hath deserted the connexion, and Art cannot supply her place. For, as Milton wisely expresses, "never can true reconcilement grow, where wounds of deadly hate have pierc'd so deep." [24]

Every quiet method for peace hath been ineffectual. Our prayers have been rejected with disdain; and only tended to convince us, that nothing flatters vanity, or confirms obstinacy in Kings more than repeated petitioning—and nothing hath contributed more than that very measure to make the Kings of Europe absolute: Witness Denmark and Sweden.[25] Wherefore, since nothing but blows will do, for God's sake, let us come to a final separation, and not leave the next generation to be cutting throats, under the violated unmeaning names of parent and child.

To say, they will never attempt it again is idle and visionary, we thought so at the repeal of the stamp-act, yet a year or two undeceived us; [26] as well may we suppose that nations, which have been once defeated, will never renew the quarrel.

As to government matters, it is not in the power of Britain to do this continent justice: The business of it will soon be too weighty, and intricate, to be managed with any tolerable degree of convenience, by a power so distant from us, and so very ignorant of us; for if they cannot conquer us, they cannot govern us. To be always running three or four thousand miles with a tale or a petition, waiting four or five months for an answer, which when obtained requires five or six more to explain it in, will in a few years be looked upon as folly and childishness—There was a time when it was proper, and there is a proper time for it to cease.

Small islands not capable of protecting themselves, are the proper objects for kingdoms to take under their care; but there is something very absurd, in supposing a continent to be perpetually governed by an island. In no instance hath nature made the satellite larger than its primary planet, and as England and America, with respect to each other, reverses the common order of nature, it is evident they belong to different systems; England to Europe, America to itself.

I am not induced by motives of pride, party, or resentment to espouse the doctrine of separation and independance; I am clearly, positively, and conscientiously persuaded that it is the true interest of this continent to be so; that every thing short of *that* is mere patchwork, that it can afford no lasting felicity,—that it is leaving the sword to our children, and shrinking back at a time, when, a little more, a little farther, would have rendered this continent the glory of the earth.

As Britain hath not manifested the least inclination towards a compromise, we may be assured that no terms can be obtained worthy the acceptance of the continent, or any ways equal to the expence of blood and treasure we have been already put to.[27]

The object, contended for, ought always to bear some just proportion to the expence. The removal of North, or the whole detestable junto, is a matter unworthy the millions we have expended.[28] A temporary stoppage of trade, was an inconvenience, which would have sufficiently balanced the repeal of all the acts complained of, had such repeals been obtained; but if the whole continent must take up arms, if every man must be a soldier, it is scarcely worth our while to fight against a contemptible ministry only. Dearly, dearly, do we pay for the repeal of the acts, if that is all we fight for; for in a just estimation, it is as great a folly to pay a Bunker-hill price for law, as for land. As I have always considered the independancy of this continent, as an event, which sooner or later must arrive, so from the late rapid progress of the continent to maturity, the event could not be far off. Wherefore, on the breaking out of hostilities, it was not worth while to have disputed a matter, which time would have finally redressed, unless we meant to be in earnest; otherwise, it is like wasting an estate on a suit at law, to regulate the trespasses of a tenant, whose lease is just expiring. No man was a warmer wisher for reconciliation than myself, before the fatal nineteenth of April 1775,* but the moment the event of that day was made known, I rejected

* Massacre at Lexington.

the hardened, sullen tempered Pharaoh of England for ever; and disdain the wretch, that with the pretended title of FATHER OF HIS PEOPLE can unfeelingly hear of their slaughter, and composedly sleep with their blood upon his soul.

But admitting that matters were now made up, what would be the event? I answer, the ruin of the continent. And that for several reasons.

First. The powers of governing still remaining in the hands of the king, he will have a negative over the whole legislation of this continent.[29] And as he hath shewn himself such an inveterate enemy to liberty, and discovered such a thirst for arbitrary power; is he, or is he not, a proper man to say to these colonies, *"You shall make no laws but what I please."* And is there any inhabitant in America so ignorant, as not to know, that according to what is called the *present constitution*, that this continent can make no laws but what the king gives leave to; and is there any man so unwise, as not to see, that (considering what has happened) he will suffer no law to be made here, but such as suit *his* purpose. We may be as effectually enslaved by the want of laws in America, as by submitting to laws made for us in England. After matters are made up (as it is called) can there be any doubt, but the whole power of the crown will be exerted, to keep this continent as low and humble as possible? Instead of going forward we shall go backward, or be perpetually quarrelling or ridiculously petitioning.—We are already greater than the king wishes us to be, and will he not hereafter endeavour to make us less? To bring the matter to one point. Is the power who is jealous of our prosperity, a proper power to govern us? Whoever says *No* to this question, is an *independant*, for independancy means no more, than, whether we shall make our own laws, or whether the king, the greatest enemy this continent hath, or can have, shall tell us "*there shall be no laws but such as I like.*"

But the king you will say has a negative in England; the people there can make no laws without his consent.[30] In point of right and good order, there is something very ridiculous, that a youth of twenty-one (which hath often happened) shall say to several millions of people, older and wiser than himself, I forbid this or that act of yours to be law. But in this place I decline this sort of reply, though I will never cease to expose the absurdity of it, and only answer, that England being the King's residence, and America not so, makes quite another case. The king's negative *here* is ten times more dangerous and fatal than it can be in England, for *there* he will scarcely refuse his consent to a bill for putting England into as strong a state of defence as possible, and in America he would never suffer such a bill to be passed.

America is only a secondary object in the system of British politics, England consults the good of *this* country, no farther than it answers her *own* purpose. Wherefore, her own interest leads her to suppress the growth of *ours* in every case which doth not promote her advantage, or in the least interferes with it. A pretty state we should soon be in under such a secondhand government, considering what has happened! Men do not change from enemies to friends by the alteration of a name: And in order to shew that reconciliation *now* is a dangerous doctrine, I affirm, *that it would be policy in the king at this time, to repeal the acts for the sake of reinstating himself in the government of the provinces;* in order, that HE MAY ACCOMPLISH BY CRAFT AND SUBTILTY, IN THE LONG RUN, WHAT HE CANNOT DO BY FORCE AND VIOLENCE IN THE SHORT ONE. Reconciliation and ruin are nearly related.

Secondly. That as even the best terms, which we can expect to obtain, can amount to no more than a temporary expedient, or a kind of government by guardianship, which can last no longer than till the colonies come of age, so the general face and state of things, in the interim, will be unsettled and unpromising. Emigrants of property will not choose to come to a country whose form of government hangs but by a thread, and who is every day tottering on the brink of commotion and disturbance; and numbers of the present inhabitants would lay hold of the interval, to dispose of their effects, and quit the continent.

But the most powerful of all arguments, is, that nothing but independance, i. e. a continental form of government, can keep the peace of the continent and preserve it inviolate from civil wars. I dread the event of a reconciliation with Britain now, as it is more than probable, that it will be followed by a revolt somewhere or other, the consequences of which may be far more fatal than all the malice of Britain.

Thousands are already ruined by British barbarity; (thousands more will probably suffer the same fate) Those men have other feelings than us who have nothing suffered. All they *now* possess is liberty, what they before enjoyed is sacrificed to its service, and having nothing more to lose, they disdain submission. Besides, the general temper of the colonies, towards a British government, will be like that of a youth, who is nearly out of his time; they will care very little about her. And a government which cannot preserve the peace, is no government at all, and in that case we pay our money for nothing; and pray what is it that Britain can do, whose power will be wholly on paper, should a civil tumult break out the very day after reconciliation? I have heard some men say, many of whom I believe spoke without thinking, that they dreaded an independance, fearing that it would produce civil wars. It is but seldom that our first thoughts are truly correct, and that is the case here; for there are ten times more to dread from a patched up connexion than from independance. I make the sufferers case my own, and I protest, that were I driven from house and home, my property destroyed, and my circumstances ruined, that as man, sensible of injuries, I could never relish the doctrine of reconciliation, or consider myself bound thereby.

The colonies have manifested such a spirit of good order and obedience to continental government, as is sufficient to make every reasonable person easy and happy on that head. No man can assign the least pretence for his fears, on any other grounds, than such as are truly childish and ridiculous, viz. that one colony will be striving for superiority over another.

Where there are no distinctions there can be no superiority, perfect equality affords no temptation. The republics of Europe are all (and we may say always) in peace. Holland and Swisserland are without wars, foreign or domestic: Monarchical governments, it is true, are never long at rest; the crown itself is a temptation to enterprizing ruffians at *home;* and that degree of pride and insolence ever attendant on regal authority, swells into a rupture with foreign powers, in instances, where a republican government, by being formed on more natural principles, would negotiate the mistake.

If there is any true cause of fear respecting independance, it is because no plan is yet laid down. Men do not see their way out—Wherefore, as an opening into that business, I offer the following hints; at the same time modestly affirming, that I have no other opinion of them myself, than that they may be the means of giving rise to something better. Could the straggling thoughts of individuals be collected, they would frequently form materials for wise and able men to improve into useful matter.

Let the assemblies be annual, with a President only. The representation more equal. Their business wholly domestic, and subject to the authority of a Continental Congress.

Let each colony be divided into six, eight, or ten, convenient districts, each district to send a proper number of delegates to Congress, so that each colony send at least thirty. The whole number in Congress will be at least 390. Each Congress to sit and to choose a president by the following method. When the delegates are met, let a colony be taken from the whole thirteen colonies by lot, after which, let the whole Congress choose (by ballot) a president from out of the delegates of *that* province. In the next Congress, let a colony be taken by lot from twelve only, omitting that colony from which the president was taken in the former Congress, and so proceeding on till the whole thirteen shall have had their proper rotation. And in order that nothing may pass into a law but what is satisfactorily just, not less than three fifths of the Congress to be called a majority—He that will promote discord, under a government so equally formed as this, would have joined Lucifer in his revolt.

But as there is a peculiar delicacy, from whom, or in what manner, this business must first arise, and as it seems most agreeable and consistent, that it should come from some intermediate body between the governed and the governors, that is, between the Congress and the people, let a CONTINENTAL CONFERENCE be held, in the following manner, and for the following purpose.

A committee of twenty-six members of Congress, viz. two for each colony. Two Members from each House of Assembly, or Provincial Convention; and five representatives of the people at large, to be chosen in the capital city or town of each province, for and in behalf of the whole province, by as many qualified voters as shall think proper to attend from all parts of the province for that purpose; or, if more convenient, the representatives may be chosen in two or three of the most populous parts thereof. In this conference, thus assembled, will be united, the two grand principles of business *knowledge* and *power*. The members of Congress, Assemblies, or Conventions, by having had experience in national concerns, will be able and useful counsellors, and the whole, being impowered by the people, will have a truly legal authority.

The conferring members being met, let their business be to frame a CONTINENTAL CHARTER, or Charter of the United Colonies; (answering to what is called the Magna Charta of England) fixing the number and manner of choosing members of Congress, members of Assembly, with their date of sitting, and drawing the line of business and jurisdiction between them: (Always remembering, that our strength is continental, not provincial:) Securing freedom and property to all men, and above all things, the free exercise of religion, according to the dictates of conscience; with such other matter as is necessary for a charter to contain. Immediately after which, the said Conference to dissolve, and the bodies which shall be chosen comformable to the said charter, to be the legislators and governors of this continent for the time being: Whose peace and happiness may God preserve, Amen.

Should any body of men be hereafter delegated for this or some similar purpose, I offer them the following extracts from that wise observer on governments *Dragonetti*. "The science" says he "of the politician consists in fixing the true point of happiness and freedom. Those men would deserve the gratitude of ages, who should discover a mode of government that contained the greatest sum of individual happiness, with the least national expence.

Dragonetti on virtue and rewards." [31]

But where, says some, is the King of America? I'll tell you. Friend, he reigns above, and doth not make havoc of mankind like the Royal Brute of Britain. Yet that we may not appear to be defective even in earthly honors, let a day be solemnly set apart for proclaiming the charter; let it be brought forth placed on the divine law, the word of God; let a crown be placed thereon, by which the world may know, that so far we approve of monarchy, that in America THE LAW IS KING. For as in absolute governments the King is law, so in free countries the law *ought* to be King; and there ought to be no other. But lest any ill use should afterwards arise, let the crown at the conclusion of the ceremony, be demolished, and scattered among the people whose right it is.

A government of our own is our natural right: And when a man seriously reflects on the precariousness of human affairs, he will become convinced, that it is infinitely wiser and safer, to form a constitution of our own in a cool deliberate manner, while we have it in our power, than to trust such an interesting event to time and chance. If we omit it now, some * Massanello may hereafter arise, who laying hold of popular disquietudes, may collect together the desperate and the discontented, and by assuming to themselves the powers of government, may sweep away the liberties of the continent like a deluge.[32] Should the government of America return again into the hands of Britain, the tottering situation of things will be a temptation for some desperate adventurer to try his fortune; and in such a case, what relief can Britain give? Ere she could hear the news, the fatal business might be done; and ourselves suffering like the wretched Britons under the oppression of the Conqueror. Ye that oppose independance now, ye know not what ye do; ye are opening a

* Thomas Anello otherwise Massanello a fisherman of Naples, who after spiriting up his countrymen in the public market-place, against the oppressions of the Spaniards, to whom the place was then subject prompted them to revolt, and in the space of a day became king.

door to eternal tyranny, by keeping vacant the seat of government. There are thousands, and tens of thousands, who would think it glorious to expel from the continent that barbarous and hellish power, which hath stirred up the Indians and Negroes to destroy us; the cruelty hath a double guilt, it is dealing brutally by us, and treacherously by them.

To talk of friendship with those in whom our reason forbids us to have faith, and our affections wounded through a thousand pores instruct us to detest, is madness and folly. Every day wears out the little remains of kindred between us and them, and can there be any reason to hope, that as the relationship expires, the affection will increase, or that we shall agree better, when we have ten times more and greater concerns to quarrel over than ever?

Ye that tell us of harmony and reconciliation, can ye restore to us the time that is past? Can ye give to prostitution its former innocence? Neither can ye reconcile Britain and America. The last cord now is broken, the people of England are presenting addresses against us. There are injuries which nature cannot forgive; she would cease to be nature if she did. As well can the lover forgive the ravisher of his mistress, as the continent forgive the murders of Britain. The Al-

mighty hath implanted in us these unextinguish-
able feelings for good and wise purposes. They
are the guardians of his image in our hearts. They
distinguish us from the herd of common animals.
The social compact would dissolve, and justice be
extirpated the earth, or have only a casual existence were we callous to the touches of affection.
The robber, and the murderer, would often es-
cape unpunished, did not the injuries which our
tempers sustain, provoke us into justice.

O ye that love mankind! Ye that dare oppose,
not only the tyranny, but the tyrant, stand forth!
Every spot of the old world is overrun with oppression. Freedom hath been hunted round the
globe. Asia, and Africa, have long expelled her—
Europe regards her like a stranger, and England
hath given her warning to depart. O! receive the
fugitive, and prepare in time an asylum for mankind.

Of the present ABILITY of AMERICA, with some miscellaneous REFLEXIONS

I have never met with a man, either in England
or America, who hath not confessed his opinion,
that a separation between the countries, would
take place one time or other: And there is no instance, in which we have shewn less judgment,

than in endeavouring to describe, what we call the ripeness or fitness of the Continent for independance.

As all men allow the measure, and vary only in their opinion of the time, let us, in order to remove mistakes, take a general survey of things, and endeavour, if possible, to find out the *very* time. But we need not go far, the inquiry ceases at once, for, the *time hath found us*. The general concurrence, the glorious union of all things prove the fact.

It is not in numbers, but in unity, that our great strength lies; yet our present numbers are sufficient to repel the force of all the world. The Continent hath, at this time, the largest body of armed and disciplined men of any power under Heaven; and is just arrived at that pitch of strength, in which no single colony is able to support itself, and the whole, when united, can accomplish the matter, and either more, or, less than this, might be fatal in its effects. Our land force is already sufficient, and as to naval affairs, we cannot be insensible, that Britain would never suffer an American man of war to be built, while the continent remained in her hands. Wherefore, we should be no forwarder an hundred years hence in that branch, than we are now; but the truth is, we should be less so, because the timber of the country is every day diminishing, and that, which will remain at last, will be far off and difficult to procure.

Were the continent crowded with inhabitants, her sufferings under the present circumstances would be intolerable. The more seaport towns we had, the more should we have both to defend and to lose. Our present numbers are so happily proportioned to our wants, that no man need be idle. The diminution of trade affords an army, and the necessities of an army create a new trade.

Debts we have none; and whatever we may contract on this account will serve as a glorious momento of our virtue. Can we but leave posterity with a settled form of government, an independant constitution of its own, the purchase at any price will be cheap. But to expend millions for the sake of getting a few vile acts repealed, and routing the present ministry only, is unworthy the charge, and is using posterity with the utmost cruelty; because it is leaving them the great work to do, and a debt upon their backs, from which they derive no advantage. Such a thought is unworthy a man of honor, and is the true characteristic of a narrow heart and a peddling politician.

The debt we may contract doth not deserve our regard, if the work be but accomplished. No nation ought to be without a debt. A national debt is a national bond; and when it bears no interest, is in no case a grievance. Britain is oppressed with a debt of upwards of one hundred and forty millions sterling, for which she pays upwards of four millions interest. And as a compensation for her debt, she has a large navy; America is without a debt, and without a navy; yet for the twentieth part of the English national debt, could have a navy as large again. The navy of England is not worth, at this time, more than three millions and an half sterling.

The first and second editions of this pamphlet were published without the following calculations, which are now given as a proof that the above estimation of the navy is a just one. *See Entic's naval history, intro.* page 56.[33]

The charge of building a ship of each rate, and furnishing her with masts, yards, sails and rigging, together with a proportion of eight months boatswain's and carpenter's seastores, as calculated by Mr. Burchett, Secretary to the navy.[34]

				£.
For a ship of a 100 guns	—			35,553
90	—	—		29,886
80	—	—		23,638

70	—	—	17,785
60	—	—	14,197
50	—	—	10,606
40	—	—	7,558
30	—	—	5,846
20	—	—	3,710

And from hence it is easy to sum up the value, or cost rather, of the whole British navy, which in the year 1757, when it was at its greatest glory consisted of the following ships and guns:

Ships.	Guns.	Cost of one.	Cost of all.
6 —	100 —	35,553*l*. ——	213,318*l*.
12 —	90 —	29,886 ——	358,632
12 —	80 —	23,638 ——	283,656
43 —	70 —	17,785 ——	764,755
35 —	60 —	14,197 ——	496,895
40 —	50 —	10,606 ——	424,240
45 —	40 —	7,558 ——	340,110
58 —	20 —	3,710 ——	215,180
85	Sloops, bombs, and fireships, one with another,	2,000	170,000
		Cost	3,266,786
	Remains for guns,	——	233,214
			3,500,000

No country on the globe is so happily situated, or so internally capable of raising a fleet as America. Tar, timber, iron, and cordage are her natural produce. We need go abroad for nothing. Whereas the Dutch, who make large profits by hiring out their ships of war to the Spaniards and Portuguese, are obliged to import most of their materials they use. We ought to view the building a fleet as an article of commerce, it being the natural manufactory of this country. It is the best money we can lay out. A navy when finished is worth more than it cost. And is that nice point in national policy, in which commerce and protection are united. Let us build; if we want them not, we can sell; and by that means replace our paper currency with ready gold and silver.

In point of manning a fleet, people in general run into great errors; it is not necessary that one fourth part should be sailors. The Terrible privateer, Captain Death, stood the hottest engagement of any ship last war, yet had not twenty sailors on board, though her complement of men was upwards of two hundred.[35] A few able and social sailors will soon instruct a sufficient number of active landmen in the common work of a ship. Wherefore, we never can be more capable to begin on maritime matters than now, while our timber is standing, our fisheries blocked up, and our sailors and shipwrights out of employ. Men of war of seventy and eighty guns were built forty years ago in New-England, and why not the same now? Ship-building is America's greatest pride, and in which she will in time excel the whole world. The great empires of the east are mostly inland, and consequently excluded from the possibility of rivalling her. Africa is in a state of barbarism; and no power in Europe hath either such an extent of coast, or such an internal supply of materials. Where nature hath given the one, she has withheld the other; to America only hath she been liberal of both. The vast empire of Russia is almost shut out from the sea: wherefore, her boundless forests, her tar, iron, and cordage are only articles of commerce.

In point of safety, ought we to be without a fleet? We are not the little people now, which we were sixty years ago; at that time we might have trusted our property in the streets, or fields rather; and slept securely without locks or bolts to our doors or windows. The case now is altered, and our methods of defence ought to improve with our increase of property. A common pirate, twelve months ago, might have come up the Delaware, and laid the city of Philadelphia under instant contribution, for what sum he pleased; and the same might have happened to other places. Nay, any daring fellow, in a brig of fourteen or sixteen guns might have robbed the whole continent, and carried off half a million of money. These are circumstances which demand our attention, and point out the necessity of naval protection.

Some, perhaps, will say, that after we have made it up with Britain, she will protect us. Can we be so unwise as to mean, that she shall keep a navy in our harbours for that purpose? Common sense will tell us, that the power which hath endeavoured to subdue us, is of all others the most improper to defend us. Conquest may be effected under the pretence of friendship; and ourselves after a long and brave resistance, be at last cheated into slavery. And if her ships are not to be admitted into our harbours, I would ask, how is she to protect us? A navy three or four thousand miles off can be of little use, and on sudden emergencies, none at all. Wherefore, if we must hereafter protect ourselves, why not do it for ourselves? Why do it for an other?

The English list of ships of war, is long and formidable, but not a tenth part of them are at any one time fit for service, numbers of them not in being; yet their names are pompously continued in the list, if only a plank be left of the ship: and not a fifth part of such as are fit for service, can be spared on any one station at one time. The East and West Indies, Mediterranean, Africa, and other parts over which Britain extends her claim, make large demands upon her navy. From a mixture of prejudice and inattention, we have contracted a false notion respecting the navy of England, and have talked as if we should have the whole of it to encounter at once, and for that reason, supposed, that we must have one as large; which not being instantly practicable, have been made use of by a set of disguised Tories to discourage our beginning thereon. Nothing can be farther from truth than this; for if America had only a twentieth part of the naval force of Britain, she would be by far an overmatch for her; because, as we neither have, nor claim any foreign dominion, our whole force would be employed on our own coast, where we should, in the long run, have two to one the advantage of those who had three or four thousand miles to sail over, before they could attack us, and the same distance to return in order to refit and recruit. And although Britain, by her fleet, hath a check over our trade to Europe, we have as large a one over her trade to the West-Indies, which, by laying in the neighbourhood of the continent, is entirely at its mercy.

Some method might be fallen on to keep up a naval force in time of peace, if we should not judge it necessary to support a constant navy. If premiums were to be given to merchants, to build and employ in their service ships mounted with twenty, thirty, forty or fifty guns, (the premiums to be in proportion to the loss of bulk to the merchants) fifty or sixty of those ships, with a few guardships on constant duty, would keep up a sufficient navy, and that without burdening ourselves with the evil so loudly complained of in England, of suffering their fleet, in time of peace to lie rotting in the docks. To unite the sinews of commerce and defence is sound policy; for when our strength and our riches play into each other's hand, we need fear no external enemy.

In almost every article of defence we abound. Hemp flourishes even to rankness, so that we need not want cordage. Our iron is superior to that of other countries. Our small arms equal to any in the world. Cannon we can cast at pleasure. Saltpetre and gunpowder we are every day producing. Our knowledge is hourly improving. Resolution is our inherent character, and courage hath never yet forsaken us. Wherefore, what is it that we want? Why is it that we hesitate? From Britain we can expect nothing but ruin. If she is once admitted to the government of America again, this Continent will not be worth living in. Jealousies will be always arising; insurrections will be constantly happening; and who will go forth to quell them? Who will venture his life to reduce his own countrymen to a foreign obedience? The difference between Pennsylvania and

Connecticut, respecting some unlocated lands, shews the insignificance of a British government, and fully proves, that nothing but Continental authority can regulate Continental matters.

Another reason why the present time is preferable to all others, is, that the fewer our numbers are, the more land there is yet unoccupied, which instead of being lavished by the king on his worthless dependants, may be hereafter applied, not only to the discharge of the present debt, but to the constant support of government. No nation under heaven hath such an advantage at this.

The infant state of the Colonies, as it is called, so far from being against, is an argument in favor of independance. We are sufficiently numerous, and were we more so, we might be less united. It is a matter worthy of observation, that the more a country is peopled, the smaller their armies are. In military numbers, the ancients far exceeded the moderns: and the reason is evident, for trade being the consequence of population, men become too much absorbed thereby to attend to any thing else. Commerce diminishes the spirit, both of patriotism and military defence. And history sufficiently informs us, that the bravest achievements were always accomplished in the non-age of a nation. With the increase of commerce, England hath lost its spirit. The city of London, notwith-

standing its numbers, submits to continued insults
with the patience of a coward. The more men have
to lose, the less willing are they to venture. The
rich are in general slaves to fear, and submit to
courtly power with the trembling duplicity of a
Spaniel.

Youth is the seed time of good habits, as well
in nations as in individuals. It might be difficult,
if not impossible, to form the Continent into one
government half a century hence. The vast variety of interests, occasioned by an increase of
trade and population, would create confusion.
Colony would be against colony. Each being able
might scorn each other's assistance: and while the
proud and foolish gloried in their little distinctions, the wise would lament, that the union had
not been formed before. Wherefore, the *present
time* is the *true time* for establishing it. The in-
timacy which is contracted in infancy, and the
friendship which is formed in misfortune, are, of
all others, the most lasting and unalterable. Our
present union is marked with both these characters: we are young, and we have been distressed;
but our concord hath withstood our troubles, and
fixes a memorable æra for posterity to glory in.

The present time, likewise, is that peculiar time,
which never happens to a nation but once, *viz.* the
time of forming itself into a government. Most

nations have let slip the opportunity, and by that means have been compelled to receive laws from their conquerors, instead of making laws for themselves. First, they had a king, and then a form of government; whereas, the articles or charter of government, should be formed first, and men delegated to execute them afterward: but from the errors of other nations, let us learn wisdom, and lay hold of the present opportunity——*To begin government at the right end.*

When William the Conqueror subdued England, he gave them law at the point of the sword; and until we consent, that the seat of government, in America, be legally and authoritatively occupied, we shall be in danger of having it filled by some fortunate ruffian, who may treat us in the same manner, and then, where will be our freedom? where our property?

As to religion, I hold it to be the indispensable duty of all government, to protect all conscientious professors thereof, and I know of no other business which government hath to do therewith, Let a man throw aside that narrowness of soul, that selfishness of principle, which the niggards of all professions are so unwilling to part with, and he will be at once delivered of his fears on that head. Suspicion is the companion of mean souls, and the bane of all good society. For myself, I fully and conscientiously believe, that it is the will of the Almighty, that there should be diversity of religious opinions among us: It affords a larger field for our Christian kindness. Were we all of one way of thinking, our religious dispositions would want matter for probation; and on this liberal principle, I look on the various denominations among us, to be like children of the same family, differing only, in what is called, their Christian names.

In page forty,[36] I threw out a few thoughts on the propriety of a Continental Charter, (for I only presume to offer hints, not plans) and in this place, I take the liberty of rementioning the subject, by observing, that a charter is to be understood as a bond of solemn obligation, which the whole enters into, to support the right of every separate part, whether of religion, personal freedom, or property. A firm bargain and a right reckoning make long friends.

In a former page I likewise mentioned the necessity of a large and equal representation; and there is no political matter which more deserves our attention. A small number of electors, or a small number of representatives, are equally dangerous. But if the number of the representatives be not only small, but unequal, the danger is increased. As an instance of this, I mention the

following; when the Associators petition was before the House of Assembly of Pennsylvania;
twenty-eight members only were present, all the
Bucks county members, being eight, voted against
it, and had seven of the Chester members done
the same, this whole province had been governed
by two counties only, and this danger it is always
exposed to. The unwarrantable stretch likewise,
which that house made in their last sitting, to
gain an undue authority over the Delegates of
that province, ought to warn the people at large,
how they trust power out of their own hands. A
set of instructions for the Delegates were put together, which in point of sense and business would
have dishonored a schoolboy, and after being approved by a *few*, a *very few* without doors, were
carried into the House, and there passed *in behalf
of the whole colony;* [37] whereas, did the whole
colony know, with what ill-will that House hath
entered on some necessary public measures, they
would not hesitate a moment to think them unworthy of such a trust.

Immediate necessity makes many things convenient, which if continued would grow into oppressions. Expedience and right are different
things. When the calamities of America required
a consultation, there was no method so ready, or
at that time so proper, as to appoint persons from
the several Houses of Assembly for that purpose;

and the wisdom with which they have proceeded hath preserved this continent from ruin. But as it is more than probable that we shall never be without a CONGRESS, every well wisher to good order, must own, that the mode for choosing members of that body, deserves consideration. And I put it as a question to those, who make a study of mankind, whether *representation and election* is not too great a power for one and the same body of men to possess? When we are planning for posterity, we ought to remember, that virtue is not hereditary.

It is from our enemies that we often gain excellent maxims, and are frequently surprised into reason by their mistakes, Mr. Cornwall (one of the Lords of the Treasury) treated the petition of the New-York Assembly with contempt,[38] because *that* House, he said, consisted but of twenty-six members, which trifling number, he argued, could not with decency be put for the whole. We thank him for his involuntary honesty.*

To CONCLUDE, however strange it may appear to some, or however unwilling they may be to think so, matters not, but many strong and striking reasons may be given, to shew, that nothing can settle our affairs so expeditiously as an open

* Those who would fully understand of what great consequence a large and equal representation is to a state, should read Burgh's political Disquisitions.[39]

and determined declaration for independance. Some of which are,

First.—It is the custom of nations, when any two are at war, for some other powers, not engaged in the quarrel, to step in as mediators, and bring about the preliminaries of a peace: but while America calls herself the Subject of Great-Britain, no power, however well disposed she may be, can offer her mediation. Wherefore, in our present state we may quarrel on for ever.

Secondly.—It is unreasonable to suppose, that France or Spain will give us any kind of assistance, if we mean only, to make use of that assistance for the purpose of repairing the breach, and strengthening the connection between Britain and America; because, those powers would be sufferers by the consequences.

Thirdly.—While we profess ourselves the subjects of Britain, we must, in the eye of foreign nations, be considered as rebels. The precedent is somewhat dangerous to *their peace,* for men to be in arms under the name of subjects; we, on the spot, can solve the paradox: but to unite resistance and subjection, requires an idea much too refined for common understanding.

Fourthly.—Were a manifesto to be published, and despatched to foreign courts, setting forth

the miseries we have endured, and the peaceable
methods we have ineffectually used for redress;
declaring, at the same time, that not being able,
any longer, to live happily or safely under the
cruel disposition of the British court, we had been
driven to the necessity of breaking off all connec-
tions with her; at the same time, assuring all such
courts of our peaceable disposition towards them,
and of our desire of entering into trade with
them: Such a memorial would produce more good
effects to this Continent, than if a ship were
freighted with petitions to Britain.

Under our present denomination of British
subjects, we can neither be received nor heard
abroad: The custom of all courts is against us, and
will be so, until, by an independance, we take
rank with other nations.

These proceedings may at first appear strange
and difficult; but, like all other steps which we
have already passed over, will in a little time become familiar and agreeable; and, until an independance is declared, the Continent will feel itself
like a man who continues putting off some un-
pleasant business from day to day, yet knows it
must be done, hates to set about it, wishes it over,
and is continually haunted with the thoughts of
its necessity.

APPENDIX

SINCE the publication of the first edition of this pamphlet, or rather, on the same day on which it came out, the King's Speech made its appearance in this city. Had the spirit of prophecy directed the birth of this production, it could not have brought it forth, at a more seasonable juncture, or a more necessary time. The bloody mindedness of the one, shew the necessity of pursuing the doctrine of the other. Men read by way of revenge. And the Speech, instead of terrifying, prepared a way for the manly principles of Independance.

Ceremony, and even, silence, from whatever motive they may arise, have a hurtful tendency, when they give the least degree of countenance to base and wicked performances; wherefore, if this maxim be admitted, it naturally follows, that the King's Speech, as being a piece of finished villany, deserved, and still deserves, a general execration both by the Congress and the people. Yet, as the domestic tranquillity of a nation, depends greatly, on the *chastity* of what may properly be called NATIONAL MANNERS, it is often better, to pass some things over in silent disdain, than to make use of such new methods of dislike, as might introduce the least innovation, on that guardian of our peace and safety. And, perhaps, it is chiefly owing to this prudent delicacy, that the King's Speech, hath not, before now, suffered a public execution. The Speech if it may be called one, is nothing better than a wilful audacious libel against the truth, the common good, and the existence of mankind; and is a formal and pompous method of offering up human sacrifices to the pride of tyrants. But this general massacre of mankind, is one of the privileges, and the certain consequence of Kings; for as nature knows them *not*, they know *not her*, and although they are beings of our *own* creating, they know not *us*, and are become the gods of their creators. The Speech hath one good quality, which is, that it is not calculated to deceive, neither can we, even if we would, be deceived by it. Brutality and tyranny appear on the face of it. It leaves us at no loss: And every line convinces, even in the moment of reading, that He, who hunts the woods for prey, the naked and untutored Indian, is less a Savage than the King of Britain.

Sir John Dalrymple, the putative father of a whining jesuitical piece, fallaciously called, "*The*

Address of the people of ENGLAND *to the inhabitants of* AMERICA," [40] hath, perhaps, from a vain supposition, that the people *here* were to be frightened at the pomp and description of a king, given, (though very unwisely on his part) the real character of the present one: "But," says this writer, "if you are inclined to pay compliments to an administration, which we do not complain of," (meaning the Marquis of Rockingham's at the repeal of the Stamp Act) "it is very unfair in you to withhold them from that prince, *by whose* NOD ALONE *they were permitted to do any thing.*" This is toryism with a witness! Here is idolatry even without a mask: And he who can calmly hear, and digest such doctrine, hath forfeited his claim to rationality—an apostate from the order of manhood; and ought to be considered—as one, who hath not only given up the proper dignity of man, but sunk himself beneath the rank of animals, and contemptibly crawl through the world like a worm.

However, it matters very little now, what the king of England either says or does; he hath wickedly broken through every moral and human obligation, trampled nature and conscience beneath his feet; and by a steady and constitutional spirit of insolence and cruelty, procured for himself an universal hatred. It is *now* the interest of America to provide for herself. She hath already a large and young family, whom it is more her duty to take care of, than to be granting away her property, to support a power who is become a reproach to the names of men and christians—YE, whose office it is to watch over the morals of a nation, of whatsoever sect or denomination ye are of, as well as ye, who, are more immediately the guardians of the public liberty, if ye wish to preserve your native country uncontaminated by European corruption, ye must in secret wish a separation—But leaving the moral part to private reflection, I shall chiefly confine my farther remarks to the following heads.

First. That it is the interest of America to be separated from Britain.

Secondly. Which is the easiest and most practicable plan, RECONCILIATION OR INDEPENDANCE? with some occasional remarks.

In support of the first, I could, if I judged it proper, produce the opinion of some of the ablest and most experienced men on this continent; and whose sentiments, on that head, are not yet publicly known. It is in reality a self-evident position: For no nation in a state of foreign dependance, limited in its commerce, and cramped and fettered in its legislative powers, can ever arrive at any material eminence. America doth not yet know what opulence is; and although the progress which she hath made stands unparalleled in the history of other nations, it is but childhood, compared with what she would be capable of arriving at, had she, as she ought to have, the legislative powers in her own hands. England is, at this time, proudly coveting what would do her no good, were she to accomplish it; and the Continent hesitating on a matter, which will be her final ruin if neglected. It is the commerce and not the conquest of America, by which England is to be benefited, and that would in a great measure continue, were the countries as independant of each other as France and Spain; because in many articles, neither can go to a better market. But it is the independance of this country on Britain or any other, which is now the main and only object worthy of contention, and which, like all other truths discovered by necessity, will appear clearer and stronger every day.

First. Because it will come to that one time or other.

Secondly. Because, the longer it is delayed the harder it will be to accomplish.

I have frequently amused myself both in public and private companies, with silently remarking, the specious errors of those who speak without reflecting. And among the many which I have heard, the following seems the most general, viz. that had this rupture happened forty or fifty years hence, instead of *now*, the Continent would have been more able to have shaken off the dependance. To which I reply, that our military ability, *at this time*, arises from the experience gained in the last war, and which in forty or fifty years time, would have been totally extinct. The Continent, would not, by that time, have had a General, or even a military officer left; and we, or those who may succeed us, would have been as ignorant of martial matters as the ancient Indians: And this single position, closely attended to, will unanswerably prove, that the present time is preferable to all others. The argument turns thus—at the conclusion of the last war, we had experience, but wanted numbers; and forty or fifty years hence, we should have numbers, without experience; wherefore, the proper point of time, must be some particular point between the two extremes, in which a sufficiency of the former remains, and a proper increase of the latter is obtained: And that point of time is the present time.

The reader will pardon this digression, as it does not properly come under the head I first set out with, and to which I again return by the following position, viz.

Should affairs be patched up with Britain, and she to remain the governing and sovereign power

of America, (which, as matters are now circum-
stanced, is giving up the point entirely) we shall
deprive ourselves of the very means of sinking
the debt we have, or may contract. The value of
the back lands which some of the provinces are
clandestinely deprived of, by the unjust extension
of the limits of Canada,[41] valued only at five
pounds sterling per hundred acres, amount to upwards of twenty-five millions, Pennsylvania currency; and the quit-rents at one penny sterling
per acre, to two millions yearly.

It is by the sale of those lands that the debt
may be sunk, without burthen to any, and the
quit-rent reserved thereon, will always lessen, and
in time, will wholly support the yearly expence
of government. It matters not how long the debt
is in paying, so that the lands when sold be applied to the discharge of it, and for the execution
of which, the Congress for the time being, will
be the continental trustees.

I proceed now to the second head, viz. Which
is the easiest and most practicable plan, RECON-
CILIATION or INDEPENDANCE; with some occasional remarks.

He who takes nature for his guide is not easily
beaten out of his argument, and on that ground,
I answer generally—That INDEPENDANCE being a
SINGLE SIMPLE LINE, contained within ourselves;

and reconciliation, a matter exceedingly perplexed and complicated, and in which, a treacherous capricious court is to interfere, gives the answer without a doubt.

The present state of America is truly alarming to every man who is capable of reflexion. Without law, without government, without any other mode of power than what is founded on, and granted by courtesy. Held together by an unexampled concurrence of sentiment, which, is nevertheless subject to change, and which, every secret enemy is endeavouring to dissolve. Our present condition, is, Legislation without law; wisdom without a plan; a constitution without a name; and, what is strangely astonishing, perfect Independance contending for dependance. The instance is without a precedent; the case never existed before; and who can tell what may be the event? The property of no man is secure in the present unbraced system of things. The mind of the multitude is left at random, and seeing no fixed object before them, they pursue such as fancy or opinion starts. Nothing is criminal; there is no such thing as treason; wherefore, every one thinks himself at liberty to act as he pleases. The Tories dared not have assembled offensively, had they known that their lives, by that act, were forfeited to the laws of the state. A line of distinction should be drawn, between, English soldiers taken in battle, and inhabitants of America taken in arms. The first are prisoners, but the latter traitors. The one forfeits his liberty, the other his head.

Notwithstanding our wisdom, there is a visible feebleness in some of our proceedings which gives encouragement to dissensions. The Continental Belt is too loosely buckled. And if something is not done in time, it will be too late to do any thing, and we shall fall into a state, in which, neither *Reconciliation* nor *Independance* will be practicable. The king and his worthless adherents are got at their old game of dividing the Continent, and there are not wanting among us, Printers, who will be busy in spreading specious falsehoods. The artful and hypocritical letter which appeared a few months ago in two of the New-York papers, and likewise in two others, is an evidence that there are men who want either judgment or honesty.[42]

It is easy getting into holes and corners and talking of reconciliation: But do such men seriously consider, how difficult the task is, and how dangerous it may prove, should the Continent divide thereon. Do they take within their view, all the various orders of men whose situation and circumstances, as well as their own, are to be considered therein. Do they put themselves in the place of the sufferer whose *all* is *already* gone, and of the soldier, who hath quitted *all* for the defence of his country. If their ill judged moderation be suited to their own private situations *only*, regardless of others, the event will convince them, that "they are reckoning without their Host."

Put us, says some, on the footing we were on in sixty-three:[43] To which I answer, the request is not *now* in the power of Britain to comply with, neither will she propose it; but if it were, and even should be granted, I ask, as a reasonable question, By what means is such a corrupt and faithless court to be kept to its engagements? Another parliament, nay, even the present, may hereafter repeal the obligation, on the pretence, of its being violently obtained, or unwisely granted; and in that case, Where is our redress?—No going to law with nations; cannon are the barristers of Crowns; and the sword, not of justice, but of war, decides the suit. To be on the footing of sixty-three, it is not sufficient, that the laws only be put on the same state, but, that our circumstances, likewise, be put on the same state; Our burnt and destroyed towns repaired or built up, our private losses made good, our public debts (contracted for defence) discharged; otherwise, we shall be millions worse than we were at that enviable period. Such a request, had it been complied with a year ago, would have won the heart and soul of the Continent— but now it is too late, "The Rubicon is passed."

Besides, the taking up arms, merely to enforce the repeal of a pecuniary law, seems as unwarrantable by the divine law, and as repugnant to human feelings, as the taking up arms to enforce obedience thereto. The object, on either side, doth not justify the means; for the lives of men are too valuable to be cast away on such trifles. It is the violence which is done and threatened to our persons; the destruction of our property by an armed force; the invasion of our country by fire and sword, which conscientiously qualifies the use of arms: And the instant, in which such a mode of defence became necessary, all subjection to Britain ought to have ceased; and the independancy of America, should have been considered, as dating its æra from, and published by, *the first musket that was fired against her*. This line is a line of consistency; neither drawn by caprice, nor extended by ambition; but produced by a chain of events, of which the colonies were not the authors.

I shall conclude these remarks, with the following timely and well intended hints. We ought to reflect, that there are three different ways, by which an independancy may hereafter be effected; and that *one* of those *three*, will one day or other, be the fate of America, viz. By the legal voice of the people in Congress; by a military power; or by a mob: It may not always happen that our soldiers are citizens, and the multitude a body of reasonable men; virtue, as I have already remarked, is not hereditary, neither is it perpetual. Should an independancy be brought about by the first of those means, we have every opportunity and every encouragement before us, to form the noblest purest constitution on the face of the earth. We have it in our power to begin the world over again. A situation, similar to the present, hath not happened since the days of Noah until now. The birthday of a new world is at hand, and a race of men, perhaps as numerous as all Europe contains, are to receive their portion of freedom from the event of a few months. The Reflexion is awful— and in this point of view, How trifling, how ridiculous, do the little, paltry cavillings, of a few weak or interested men appear, when weighed against the business of a world.

Should we neglect the present favorable and inviting period, and an Independance be hereafter effected by any other means, we must charge the consequence to ourselves, or to those rather, whose narrow and prejudiced souls, are habitually opposing the measure, without either inquiring or reflecting. There are reasons to be given in support of Independance, which men should rather privately think of, than be publicly told of. We ought not now to be debating whether we shall be independant or not, but, anxious to accomplish it

on a firm, secure, and honorable basis, and uneasy
rather that it is not yet begau upon. Every day
convinces us of its necessity. Even the Tories (if
such beings yet remain among us) should, of all
men, be the most solicitous to promote it; for, as
the appointment of committees at first, protected
them from popular rage, so, a wise and well established form of government, will be the only
certain means of continuing it securely to them.
Wherefore, if they have not virtue enough to be
Whigs, they ought to have prudence enough to
wish for Independance.

In short, Independance is the only Bond that
can tye and keep us together. We shall then see
our object, and our ears will be legally shut
against the schemes of an intriguing, as well, as
a cruel enemy. We shall then too, be on a proper
footing, to treat with Britain; for there is reason
to conclude, that the pride of that court, will be
less hurt by treating with the American states for
terms of peace, than with those, whom she de-
nominates, "rebellious subjects," for terms of ac-
commodation. It is our delaying it that encourages her to hope for conquest, and our backward-
ness tends only to prolong the war. As we have,
without any good effect therefrom, withheld our
trade to obtain a redress of our grievances, let us
now try the alternative, by *independantly* redress-
ing them ourselves, and then offering to open

the trade. The mercantile and reasonable part in England, will be still with us; because, peace *with* trade, is preferable to war *without* it. And if this offer be not accepted, other courts may be applied to.

On these grounds I rest the matter. And as no offer hath yet been made to refute the doctrine contained in the former editions of this pamphlet, it is a negative proof, that either the doctrine cannot be refuted, or, that the party in favour of it are too numerous to be opposed. WHEREFORE, instead of gazing at each other with suspicious or doubtful curiosity, let each of us, hold out to his neighbour the hearty hand of friendship, and unite in drawing a line, which, like an act of oblivion shall bury in forgetfulness every former dissension. Let the names of Whig and Tory be extinct; and let none other be heard among us, than those of *a good citizen, an open and resolute friend, and a virtuous supporter of the* RIGHTS *of* MANKIND *and of the* FREE AND INDEPENDANT STATES OF AMERICA.

To the Representatives of the Religious Society of the People called Quakers, or to so many of them as were concerned in publishing a late piece, entitled "The ANCIENT TESTIMONY and PRINCIPLES of the People called QUAKERS renewed, with Respect to the KING and GOVERN-

MENT, and touching the COMMOTIONS now prevailing in these and other parts of AMERICA addressed to the PEOPLE IN GENERAL." [44]

The Writer of this, is one of those few, who
never dishonors religion either by ridiculing, or
cavilling at any denomination whatsoever. To
God, and not to man, are all men accountable on
the score of religion. Wherefore, this epistle is
not so properly addressed to you as a religious,
but as a political body, dabbling in matters, which
the professed Quietude of your Principles instruct
you not to meddle with.

As you have, without a proper authority for so
doing, put yourselves in the place of the whole
body of the Quakers, so, the writer of this, in
order to be on an equal rank with yourselves, is
under the necessity, of putting himself in the
place of all those, who, approve the very writings
and principles, against which, your testimony is
directed: And he hath chosen this singular situation, in order, that you might discover in him
that presumption of character which you cannot
see in yourselves. For neither he nor you can
have any claim or title to *Political Representation.*

When men have departed from the right way,
it is no wonder that they stumble and fall. And
it is evident from the manner in which ye have

managed your testimony, that politics, (as a religious body of men) is not your proper Walk; for however well adapted it might appear to you, it is, nevertheless, a jumble of good and bad put unwisely together, and the conclusion drawn therefrom, both unnatural and unjust.

The two first pages, (and the whole doth not make four) we give you credit for, and expect the same civility from you, because the love and desire of peace is not confined to Quakerism, it is the *natural*, as well the religious wish of all denominations of men. And on this ground, as men laboring to establish an Independant Constitution of our own, do we exceed all others in our hope, end, and aim. *Our plan is peace for ever*. We are tired of contention with Britain, and can see no real end to it but in a final separation. We act consistently, because for the sake of introducing an endless and uninterrupted peace, do we bear the evils and burthens of the present day. We are endeavoring, and will steadily continue to endeavor, to separate and dissolve a connexion which hath already filled our land with blood; and which, while the name of it remains, will be the fatal cause of future mischiefs to both countries.

We fight neither for revenge nor conquest; neither from pride nor passion; we are not insulting the world with our fleets and armies, nor ravaging the globe for plunder. Beneath the shade of our own vines are we attacked; in our own houses, and on our own lands, is the violence committed against us. We view our enemies in the character of Highwaymen and Housebreakers, and having no defence for ourselves in the civil law, are obliged to punish them by the military one, and apply the sword, in the very case, where you have before now, applied the halter—— Perhaps we feel for the ruined and insulted sufferers in all and every part of the continent, with a degree of tenderness which hath not yet made its way into some of your bosoms. But be ye sure that ye mistake not the cause and ground of your Testimony. Call not coldness of soul, religion; nor put the *Bigot* in the place of the *Christian*.

O ye partial ministers of your own acknowledged principles. If the bearing arms be sinful, the first going to war must be more so, by all the difference between wilful attack and unavoidable defence. Wherefore, if ye really preach from conscience, and mean not to make a political hobby-horse of your religion, convince the world thereof, by proclaiming your doctrine to our enemies, *for they likewise bear* ARMS. Give us proof of your sincerity by publishing it at St. James's, to the commanders in chief at Boston, to the Admirals and Captains who are piratically ravaging our coasts, and to all the murdering miscreants who are acting in authority under HIM whom ye profess to serve. Had ye the honest soul of * *Barclay* ye would preach repentance to *your* king; Ye would tell the Royal Wretch his sins, and warn him of eternal ruin. Ye would not spend your partial invectives against the injured and the insulted only, but, like faithful ministers, would cry aloud and *spare none*. Say not that ye are persecuted, neither endeavour to make us the authors of that reproach, which, ye are bringing upon yourselves; for we testify unto all men, that we do not complain against you because ye are *Quakers*, but because ye pretend to *be* and are NOT Quakers.

Alas! it seems by the particular tendency of some part of your testimony, and other parts of your conduct, as if, all sin was reduced to, and comprehended in, *the act of bearing arms*, and

---

* "Thou hast tasted of prosperity and adversity; thou knowest what it is to be banished thy native country, to be over-ruled as well as to rule, and set upon the throne; and being *oppressed* thou hast reason to know how *hateful* the *oppressor* is both to God and man: If after all these warnings and advertisements, thou dost not turn unto the Lord with all thy heart, but forget him who remembered thee in thy distress, and give up thyself to follow lust and vanity, surely great will be thy condemnation.—Against which snare, as well as the temptation of those who may or do feed thee, and prompt thee to evil, the most excellent and prevalent remedy will be, to apply thyself to that light of Christ which shineth in thy conscience, and which neither can, nor will flatter thee, nor suffer thee to be at ease in thy sins."

                    Barclay's Address to Charles II.[45]

that by the *people only*. Ye appear to us, to have mistaken party for conscience; because, the general tenor of your actions wants uniformity: And it is exceedingly difficult to us to give credit to many of your pretended scruples; because, we see them made by the same men, who, in the very instant that they are exclaiming against the mammon of this world, are nevertheless, hunting after it with a step as steady as Time, and an appetite as keen as Death.

The quotation which ye have made from Proverbs, in the third page of your testimony, that, "when a man's ways please the Lord, he maketh even his enemies to be at peace with him"; is very unwisely chosen on your part; because, it amounts to a proof, that the king's ways (whom ye are so desirous of supporting) do *not* please the Lord, otherwise, his reign would be in peace.

I now proceed to the latter part of your testimony, and that, for which all the foregoing seems only an introduction, viz.

"It hath ever been our judgment and principle, since we were called to profess the light of Christ Jesus, manifested in our consciences unto this day, that the setting up and putting down kings and governments, is God's peculiar prerogative; for causes best known to himself: And that it is not our business to have any hand or contrivance therein; nor to be busy bodies above our station, much less to plot and contrive the ruin, or over-turn of any of them, but to pray for the king, and safety of our nation, and good of all men: That we may live a peaceable and quiet life, in all god-liness and honesty; *under the government which God is pleased to set over us.*"—If these are *really* your principles why do ye not abide by them? Why do ye not leave that, which ye call God's Work, to be managed by himself? These very principles instruct you to wait with patience and humility, for the event of all public measures, and to receive *that event* as the divine will to-wards you. *Wherefore,* what occasion is there for your *political testimony* if you fully believe what it contains? And the very publishing it proves, that either, ye do not believe what ye profess, or have not virtue enough to practise what ye be-lieve.

The principles of Quakerism have a direct tendency to make a man the quiet and inoffensive subject of any, and every government *which is set over him.* And if the setting up and putting down of kings and governments is God's peculiar prerogative, he most certainly will not be robbed thereof by us; wherefore, the principle itself leads you to approve of every thing, which ever hap-pened, or may happen to kings as being his work.

OLIVER CROMWELL thanks you. CHARLES, then, died not by the hands of man; and should the present Proud Imitator of him, come to the same untimely end, the writers and publishers of the Testimony, are bound, by the doctrine it contains, to applaud the fact. Kings are not taken away by miracles, neither are changes in governments brought about by any other means than such as are common and human; and such as we are now using. Even the dispersion of the Jews, though foretold by our Saviour, was effected by arms. Wherefore, as ye refuse to be the means on one side, ye ought not to be meddlers on the other; but to wait the issue in silence; and unless ye can produce divine authority, to prove, that the Almighty who hath created and placed this *new* world, at the greatest distance it could possibly stand, east and west, from every part of the old, doth, nevertheless, disapprove of its being independent of the corrupt and abandoned court of Britain, unless I say, ye can shew this, how can ye on the ground of your principles, justify the exciting and stirring up the people "firmly to unite in the *abhorrence* of all such *writings*, and *measures*, as evidence a desire and design to break off the *happy* connexion we have hitherto enjoyed, with the kingdom of Great-Britain, and our just and necessary subordination to the king, and those who are lawfully placed in authority under him." What a slap of the face is here! the men, who in the very paragraph before, have quietly and passively resigned up the ordering, altering, and disposal of kings and governments, into the hands of God, are now, recalling their principles, and putting in for a share of the business. Is it possible, that the conclusion, which is here justly quoted, can any ways follow from the doctrine laid down? The inconsistency is too glaring not to be seen; the absurdity too great not to be laughed at; and such as could only have been made by those, whose understandings were darkened by the narrow and crabby spirit of a despairing political party; for ye are not to be considered as the whole body of the Quakers but only as a factional and fractional part thereof.

Here ends the examination of your testimony; (which I call upon no man to abhor, as ye have done, but only to read and judge of fairly;) to which I subjoin the following remark; "That the setting up and putting down of kings," most certainly mean, the making him a king, who is yet not so, and the making him no king who is already one. And pray what hath this to do in the present case? We neither mean to *set up* nor to *put down*, neither to *make* nor to *unmake*, but to have nothing to *do* with them. Wherefore, your testimony in whatever light it is viewed serves only to dishonor your judgment, and for many other reasons had better have been let alone than published.

First, Because it tends to the decrease and reproach of all religion whatever, and is of the utmost danger to society, to make it a party in political disputes.

Secondly, Because it exhibits a body of men,
numbers of whom disavow the publishing political testimonies, as being concerned therein and
approvers thereof.

Thirdly, Because it hath a tendency to undo
that continental harmony and friendship which
yourselves by your late liberal and charitable do-
nations hath lent a hand to establish; and the
preservation of which, is of the utmost consequence to us all.

And here without anger or resentment I bid
you farewel. Sincerely wishing, that as men and
christians, ye may always fully and uninterrupt-
edly enjoy every civil and religious right; and
be, in your turn, the means of securing it to others; but that the example which ye have unwisely
set, of mingling religion with politics, *may be
disavowed and reprobated by every inhabitant* of
America.

F I N I S .

FOOTNOTES

1. Paine's first publisher was Robert Bell of Philadelphia, who advertised the appearance of the first printing for January 9, 1776. Differences between author and publisher emerged over Bell's claim that the pamphlet had earned no profit (Paine planned to use the profits from the sale of the work for the purchase of mittens for the American troops in Canada) and his announcing a new edition before Paine had readied his material. Paine, therefore, dropped Bell and turned to William and Thomas Bradford to publish the enlarged edition, which is the edition used here. The edition was advertised for February 14. Bell promptly pirated the new material and added to it a miscellany of spirited works by other authors, calling the complete book *Large Additions to Common Sense*. The dispute, well publicized by the principles' published diatribes against one another, aided in giving *Common Sense* its great currency. For a detailed discussion and listing of the many editions of *Common Sense*, see Richard

Gimbel, *Thomas Paine, a Bibliographical Check List of Common Sense With an Account of Its Publication,* New Haven, 1956. The editor wishes to acknowledge the William L. Clements Library for its kind permission to reprint the W & T Bradford edition of *Common Sense* in its possession.

2.   Replies, however, were soon forthcoming. Among them were William Smith's "Cato" letters which appeared March 13, 1776, and John Adams' *Thoughts on Government,* April 22.

3.   The notion of government as a necessary evil, at least as old as Hobbes, was common currency among Paine's generation. "Why has government been instituted at all?" asked Hamilton in the *Federalist.* "Because," he replied, "the passions of men will not conform to the dictates of reason and justice, without constraint. . . ."

4.   In the following five paragraphs, Paine offers his version of the 17th-century theory concerning the state of nature and the origin of government, a theory perfected by John Locke in *The Second Treatise of Government,* 1690.

5.   One of the many examples in Paine's work illustrating the influence of Newtonian science upon social thought.

6. This metaphor, most notably used by Abraham Lincoln, has its origin in the Bible, Mark 3: 25.

7. Results in its own destruction. The metaphor immediately following is another illustration of the influence of mechanistic science upon Paine's thought.

8. Charles I was beheaded January 30, 1649.

9. The democratic Paine clearly is no economic leveller.

10. The English usually referred to the United Netherlands as Holland, which was the principal province of a federal republic that had its origin in the Union of Utrecht, 1579.

11. The following Biblical references are from Judges 8: 22–23 and 1 Sam. 8: 6–22; 12: 13–19.

12. An effective metaphor in an overwhelmingly Protestant America.

13. The ordinary Protestant Englishman of Paine's day lumped Mohammedanism with Catholicism as a tissue of self-serving superstitions.

14. William, illegitimate son of Robert I, Duke of Normandy, successfully invaded England and

at the Battle of Hastings killed King Harold. William was crowned King of England in the year 1066.

15. 1 Sam. 10: 31.

16. The Wars of the Roses are generally dated from 1455 (Battle of St. Albans) to 1485 (accession to the throne of Henry VII). Henry VI, around whom swirled the dynastic conflicts of the period, at nine months of age became King of England in 1422. Local insurrections in Yorkshire were successfully put down in 1489.

17. Sir William Meredith (d. 1790), Whig politician, member of Parliament, an Admiralty Lord (1765–66) during the Rockingham ministry, authored several polemical works on such issues as the Wilkes controversy and the Quebec Act.

18. Henry Pelham (1695?–1754), brother of the powerful Duke of Newcastle, was First Lord of the Treasury and Chancellor of the Exchequer from 1743–1754, the year of his death.

19. Early in the so-called Seven Years' War (or Great War for the Empire), Hanover, tied to England in the person of George II, King of England, Elector of Hanover, was overrun by French arms.

20. At mid-century, about ½ of Pennsylvania's 200,000 population was German. The other half was made up of English, Scotch-Irish, and a miscellany of other peoples.

21. The same line of argument was previously utilized by Benjamin Franklin in his satirical *Edict by the King of Prussia* (1773).

22. This principle became a fundamental doctrine of American foreign policy as it was enunciated by Washington in the Farewell Address, by Jefferson in his First Inaugural, and finally in the Monroe Doctrine.

23. Martin Luther nailed his 95 theses to the church door in Wittenberg in 1517, twenty-five years after Columbus discovered America.

24. *Paradise Lost*, IV, 99.

25. The Crown ignored John Dickinson's "Olive Branch Petition" (July 5, 1775); Gustavus III of Sweden had recently (1772) overthrown Sweden's constitution (1720) and reestablished the monarchy's former grandeur. Royal absolutism in Denmark, established in 1660, lasted until 1848.

26. The Stamp Act was repealed March, 1766; Parliament passed the Townshend duties June, 1767.

27. The Howe brothers at the Staten Island Peace Conference (September, 1776) were authorized only to offer pardons.

28. The North ministry came to office in 1770. Lord North resigned, partly as a result of Yorktown, in 1782.

29. With the exception of the two corporate colonies, Rhode Island and Connecticut, all had been required to submit their laws to the Crown for review. Some five percent of all laws submitted had been disallowed.

30. The last time that the Crown refused assent to an act of Parliament was in 1707.

31. In reply to Cesare Beccaria's famous work, *Of Crimes and Punishments* (1764), Giacinto Dragonetti wrote *On Virtues and Reward*, the first English edition appearing in London in 1767.

32. Paine here refers to Thomas Aniello, the fisherman-become-dictator of Naples in 1647 during a revolt against Spanish misrule. Masaniello, as he is also known, executed some fifteen

hundred persons before he himself was assassinated.

33. John Entick (1703?–1773), author of various works from dictionaries to polemics, published his *New Naval History* in 1757.

34. Josiah Burchett (1666?–1746), Secretary of the Admiralty, 1693–1742, and sometimes member of Parliament, wrote extensively on British naval history.

35. John Entick, *The General History of the Late War* (London, 1763), II, 110–111n, describes in detail the bloody engagement between the *Terrible* and the French frigate, the *Vengeance*, December 27, 1756. Charles Wye Kendall, *Private Men of War* (London, 1931), p. 162, further states that "out of a crew of 200 only 16 remained alive. Among the slain was the captain whose name was Death, his two lieutenants being appropriately Mr. Spirit and Mr. Ghost, whilst Mr. Butcher fulfilled the function of boatswain, and Mr. Debble that of quartermaster. Finally, to complete the lugubrious jest, the *Terrible* was launched out of Execution Dock." Paine, as he informs us in the *Rights of Man*, had personal acquaintance with the *Terrible*. At age 17, he signed aboard this privateer, an adventure from which he "was happily pre-

vented by the affectionate and moral remonstrance of a good father. . . ." (Philip Foner, ed., *The Life and Major Writings of Thomas Paine* [New York, 1945], II, 405).

36.   This edition, p. 97.

37.   On November 17, 1775, the House divided as Paine describes concerning a vote for more frequent meetings of the military association for its improvement in military discipline. *Votes of Assembly, Pennsylvania Archives,* eighth series, VIII, 7357–58. On November 9, the Assembly had instructed Pennsylvania's delegation to the Continental Congress as follows: "We strictly enjoin you, that you, in behalf of this colony, dissent from and utterly reject any propositions, should such be made, that may cause or lead to a separation from our mother country, or a change of the form of this government," *Ibid.,* VIII, 7352–53. Pennsylvania's western counties were grossly underrepresented in the Assembly.

38.   Charles Wolfram Cornwall (1735–1789) was a lord of the treasury in Lord North's government, and from 1780 to his death he was Speaker of the House of Commons.

39.   Paine's note. Bernard Bailyn, *The Ideological Origins of the American Revolution* (Cambridge, 1967), p. 41, states that Burgh's three-volume *Political Disquisitions*, published in 1774, was "the key book" of its generation in fostering the radical Whig tradition.

40.   Sir John Dalrymple (1726–1810) authored several historical and scientific works. He was for a time solicitor to the board of excise by which Paine had been employed. A later work, *The Rights of Great Britain Asserted Against The Claims of America . . .* , likewise a reply to the Continental Congress' *Declaration of the Causes and Necessity of Taking Up Arms* (July 6, 1775) has also been attributed to Dalrymple, though James Macpherson, translator of the alleged bardic epic of Ossian, is the more likely author. The present work has also been attributed to Sir William Meredith (see note 17).

41.   The Quebec Act of 1774 extended the boundaries of that province down to the Ohio River, thereby nullifying the western land claims of several colonies.

42.   Paine probably refers to a letter drafted by loyalist William Smith and signed by Governor Tryon urging the New York Assembly to con-

sider Lord North's proposals for reconciliation. The letter, dated December 4, 1775, appeared in several newspapers.

43.   The Treaty of Paris of 1763, ending the French and Indian War, marks the beginning of the series of Parliamentary enactments that led ultimately to Lexington and Concord.

44.   This cautionary address, published shortly after the appearance of *Common Sense,* was signed by John Pemberton, clerk for the Monthly Meeting of Philadelphia.

45.   Paine's note. Robert Barclay (1648–90) composed the foremost theological exposition of the Quaker faith, *An Apology for . . . the Principles and Doctrines of the People Called Quakers.* Paine refers to this work's prefatory address to the King.

BIBLIOGRAPHICAL ESSAY

Note: Asterisks indicate availability in paperback.

The study of *Common Sense* and the age of revolution from which it emerged may begin with Colonel Richard Gimbel, *Thomas Paine: A Bibliographical Check List of "Common Sense"* (1956) which details the circumstances of publication and is particularly useful for its listing of contemporary editions, variants, and replies. Perspective on the pamphlet is gained by reviewing Thomas R. Adams, *Independence: The Growth of an Idea* (1965) in which *Common Sense* appears as a culmination to the long list of pro- and anti-independence polemics published in the preceding period. Another guide, this one to Paine's life and works, is Alfred Owen Aldridge, "Thomas Paine: A Survey of Research and Criticism Since 1945," *The British Studies Monitor*, V, #2 (Winter, 1975), 3–29. For earlier studies,

Harry Hayden Clark, *Thomas Paine, Representative Selections* (2nd printing, 1961) has a lengthy topical and annotated bibliography.

Clark's book, a volume in the American Book Company's impressive *American Writer Series*, also contains the best introduction to Paine's writings, which are closely analyzed in a 127-page introduction followed by a chronology, the above mentioned bibliography, and a lengthy sampling including *Common Sense*. The standard collection of Paine's writings is Philip Foner, *The Life and Major Writings of Thomas Paine* (1948)* with which we will have to make do until it is replaced with a more accurate, scholarly, and complete edition. Doubleday Anchor Books has recently published *The Rights of Man* in tandem with Burke's *Reflections on the French Revolution* (1973)*, a useful coupling of the great protagonists of the age.

Common Sense is analyzed in R. B. Downs, *Books That Changed the World* (1956),* which examines Paine's pamphlet in company with Copernicus, Harriet Beecher Stowe, and Machiavelli, among others. More recently, the premier historians Bernard Bailyn, "Common Sense," in *Fundamental Testaments of the American Revolution* (1973), and Winthrop Jordan, "Familial Politics: Thomas Paine and the Killing of the

King, 1776," *Journal of American History*, LX (1973), 294–308, have examined Paine's pamphlet. The former probes the reasons for its unique appeal, while the latter is an ingenious exercise on the slippery ground of psychohistory. Felix Gilbert's important *To the Farewell Address: Ideas of Early American Foreign Policy* (1961)* finds a direct line from *Common Sense* to Washington's Great Rule concerning America's relations with foreign powers.

Moving from *Common Sense* to Paine's writings as a whole, Richard M. Gummere, "Thomas Paine: Was He Really Anti-Classical?" in *Seven Wise Men of Colonial America* (1967), focuses upon a narrow, though important facet of his thought. Vernon Parrington, a spirit kindred to Paine, wrote a sympathetic appreciation, "Thomas Paine: Republican Pamphleteer," in *Main Currents of American Thought*, Vol. I, *The Colonial Mind* (1927)*. The less kindred Cecelia M. Kenyon, "Where Paine Went Wrong," *American Political Science Review*, XLV (1951), 1086–1099, faults Paine's "inability to cope with the reality (self-interest, conflicts) as against the ideal of republican government." "Naive" though Paine may have been, E. P. Thompson, *The Making of the English Working Class* (1963)* shows the signal influence of Paineite rhetoric on working-class movements, a rhetoric closely analyzed by James T. Boulton, *The Language of Politics in the Age of Wilkes and Burke* (1963). The monumental study of Sir Leslie Stephen, *History of English Thought in the Eighteenth Century* (1876)* places Paine within the intellectual currents of his time. In wider perspective, Thomas W. Copeland, "Burke, Paine, and Jefferson," in *Our Eminent Friend Edmund Burke: Six Essays* (1949), while clarifying the early relationship between the two men, writes that "the great controversy in which Burke and Paine were the principal antagonists was perhaps the most crucial ideological debate ever carried on in English."

Full biographies of Paine abound. Of particular value are the following, of which the starting point is Moncure Conway, *The Life of Thomas Paine*. 2 vols. (1892). Alfred Owen Aldridge brings his profound knowledge of eighteenth-century cultural history to bear in *Man of Reason: The Life of Thomas Paine* (1959), while David Hawke, *Paine* (1974), has written the most detailed account presently available. An artful and informative short life is Crane Brinton, "Thomas Paine," in the *Dictionary of American Biography*. Eric Foner's forthcoming work is limited to Paine and America; nevertheless, it offers a fuller exploration of the sources of Paine's thought than do the full biographies presently available.

The English setting to which Foner refers is given broad yet profound study in J. H. Plumb, *England in the Eighteenth Century* (revised edition, 1963)*. Christopher Hill, *Puritanism and Revolution* (1959)* traces Paine's thought back to the seventeenth-century Levellers, while G. D. H. Cole and Raymond Postgate, *The Common People, 1746–1946* (4th edition, 1949)* throw important light on Paine's significance, particularly in Section II, "Social Movements in the Eighteenth Century." Lucy S. Sutherland, *The City of London and the Opposition to Government, 1768–1774: A Study in the Rise of Metropolitan Radicalism* (1959)* centers on the unprincipled John Wilkes. It is, however, left to Caroline Robbins, *The Eighteenth-Century Commonwealth-man* (1959)* magnificently to delineate the transit of seventeenth-century commonwealth ideas to Paine's generation.

Robbins' book represents an important school of interpretation, of which Bernard Bailyn is a preeminent master in displaying the significance of the Old Whig tradition for the American Revolution. His edition of *Pamphlets of the American Revolution, 1750–1776*, Vol. I, *1750–1765* (1965), of which inexplicably this is the only volume yet to appear, is graced by a superb essay on the sources of American revolutionary ideology, an essay which somehow appears less attractively as a separate publication, *The Ideological Origins of the American Revolution* (1967)*. Bailyn students Gordon S. Wood, *The Creation of the American Republic, 1776–1787* (1969)* and Pauline Maier, *From Resistance to Revolution: Colonial Radicals and the Development of American Opposition to Britain, 1765–1776* (1972)* respectively set Pennsylvania's revolution, in which Paine played a role, in its larger setting, and trace the radicals' increasing disenchantment with Britain. In *Benjamin Franklin and the Politics of Liberty* (1974)*, the present editor details the growing disenchantment of one such "radical" whom Paine thought of as a kind of spiritual father.

If Bailyn and his students raise revolutionary rhetoric to the expression of a pervasive ideology, Philip Davidson, *Propaganda and the American Revolution, 1763–1783* (1941)*, as his title suggests, sees it in a lesser guise. Davidson calls Paine, "agitator and propagandist supreme." Staughton Lynd, *Intellectual Origins of American Radicalism* (1968), gives Paine a prominent position in the American radical tradition, a tradition which Lynd links to both Rousseau, "who influenced America by way of England," and Marx.

A Whig ideology clearly supplied the perspective from which revolutionary Americans viewed the imperial nexus. From an institutional point of view, no one has excelled Charles Andrews, *England's Commercial and Colonial Policy*, Vol. IV, *The Colonial Period of American History* (1938)* in describing wherein the colonies were supposed to fit into the mercantile scheme. Andrews' student Mary P. Clarke, *Parliamentary Privilege in the American Colonies* (1943), examines the colonial assemblies' claims of parliamentary status while specific transatlantic disputes have been detailed in Jack P. Greene, *The Quest for Power: The Lower Houses of Assembly in the Southern Royal Colonies, 1689–1775* (1963)*. Both works in a sense provide copious annotation of Andrews' assertion that the rise of the colonial assemblies was the chief political phenomenon in American colonial history. Colonial near autonomy, as reflected in the maturation of the assemblies, helped create a dysfunction between a claimed imperial prerogative and the American political reality, a dysfunction, according to Bernard Bailyn, *The Origins of American Politics* (1968)* leading ultimately to the disruption of empire.

Merrill Jensen, *The Founding of a Nation: a History of the American Revolution, 1763–1776* (1968), turns from such general considerations to the years directly preceding independence. If Jensen's large-scale work is an example of the "progressive" inclination in American historiography —economic self-interest, not ideology motivates men (Bailyn gets not so much as a footnote)—two shorter works encapsulate respectively the so-called imperial and Whig schools of revolutionary historiography. Lawrence Gipson, *The Coming of the Revolution, 1763–1775* (1954)* is sympathetic to the British position. Bernard Knollenberg, *The Origins of the American Revolution, 1759–1766* (revised edition, 1965)*, on the other hand, arguing that revolutionary unrest preceded the year 1763, justifies in the best Whiggish tradition America's reactions to parliamentary legislation.

Particular conflicts between the mother country and the colonies may be studied in such works as Joseph A. Ernst, *Money and Politics in America, 1755–1775* (1975); Carl Ubbelohde, *The Vice-Admiralty Courts and the American Revolution* (1960); Lois Schwoerer, *"No Standing Armies!": The Antiarmy Ideology in Seventeenth Century England* (1974), which goes far to explain why the inheritors of this ideology resented the redcoats stationed among them; and David Ammerman, *In the Common Cause: American Response to the Coercive Acts of 1774* (1974).

Revolutionary Pennsylvania as Paine's adopted home is of particular importance in understanding the milieu in which the transplanted Englishman metaphorically as well as literally found himself. Charles H. Lincoln, *The Revolutionary Movement in Pennsylvania, 1760–1776* (1901), is still useful, as is Theodore Thayer, *Pennsylvania Politics and the Growth of Democracy, 1740–1776* (1953). David Hawke, *In the Midst of a Revolution* (1961)* is a detailed account of the overthrow of the Pennsylvania Assembly. John P. Selsam, *The Pennsylvania Constitution of 1776* (1936), studies the result of that action. John A. Neuenschwander in a recent book broadens his focus to *The Middle Colonies and the Coming of the American Revolution* (1974).

These colonies generally were reluctant to declare their independence. Their hesitancy may be traced in the actions—or nonactions—of their congressional delegates, as in John M. Head's enlightening book, *A Time to Rend* (1968). Edmund C. Burnet, *The Continental Congress* (1941)* is the not-so-old but nevertheless classic account of the history of Congress to 1787, but it is now significantly supplemented by H. James Henderson, *Party Politics in the Continental Congress* (1974), who, like Neuenschwander, emphasizes the sectional bases of the delegates' attitudes.

Most of these works credit Paine for his role in helping bring Congress finally to independence, of which Jefferson's Declaration is brilliantly analyzed by Carl Becker, *The Declaration of Independence* (1922)*. David Hawke, *A Transaction of Free Men: The Birth and Course of the Declaration of Independence* (1964), emphasizes the roles of individuals in the coming of independence, and, briefly, the significance of the Declaration for future generations. As for the military phase of the Revolution, while its bibliography is enormous, there is only one large-scale work that details the period between Lexington and independence: Allen French, *The First Year of the American Revolution* (1934).

Biography must not be overlooked in assessing the Revolution and Paine's role in it. Page Smith, *John Adams, 1735–1826* (1962); Clarence Ver Steeg, *Robert Morris, Revolutionary Financier* (1954); David Hawke, *Benjamin Rush: Revolutionary Gadfly* (1971); and Curtis P. Nettells, *George Washington and American Independence* (1951) concern four of the many revolutionary figures whose careers interacted with that of Paine.

The American Revolution, of course, was but one symptom of the emergence of a new political order in the Western world, a political reorientation of which Paine's revolutionary activities on two continents are symbolic. Robert Palmer's stunning *The Age of the Democratic Revolution: a*

Political History of Europe and America, 1760–1800, 2 vols. (1959 and 1964)* has given to Paine's period a new appellation. Michael Kraus, *The Atlantic Civilization: Eighteenth Century Origins* (1949)*, centers on society and culture rather than politics. Chapter IX, "America and the Utopian Ideal," is especially significant for Paine's international influence. Gwyn A. Williams, *Artisans and Sans-Culottes: Popular Movements in France and Britain During the French Revolution* (1968)* discusses the principal carriers of revolutionary infection, of which Paine's was an especially acute case.

With the exception of the typography, unfamiliar to contemporary readers (for example, "But he has protected us, fay fome," has been modernized to "But she has protected us, say some"), this edition of *Common Sense* is set in the original design of the W. & T. Bradford, Philadelphia, 1776, edition. To preserve that design, the editor's annotations have been placed at the end of the text.

The work is printed on bicentennial offset paper that is laid with the bicentennial watermark.